UNDERSTANDING
SIBLING RIVALRY
The
Brazelton Way

also by T. Berry Brazelton, M.D.

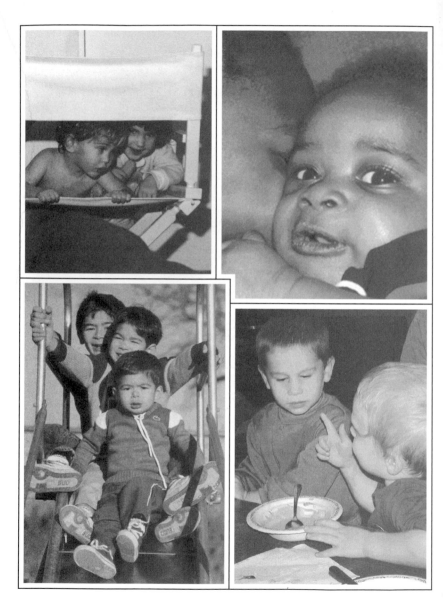

UNDERSTANDING SIBLING RIVALRY
The *Brazelton Way*

T. Berry Brazelton, M.D.
Joshua D. Sparrow, M.D.

WITHDRAWN

A Merloyd Lawrence Book

DA CAPO LIFELONG BOOKS
A Member of the Perseus Books Group

Many of the designations used by manufacturers and sellers to distinguish their products are claimed as trademarks. Where those designations appear in this book, and where Da Capo Press was aware of a trademark claim, the designations have been printed in initial capital letters.

Text design by Trish Wilkinson
Set in 11-point Adobe Garamond by the Perseus Books Group

Cataloging-in-Publication data for this book is available from the Library of Congress.

First Da Capo Press edition 2005
ISBN 0-7382-1005-6

Published by Da Capo Press
A Member of the Perseus Books Group
www.dacapopress.com

Da Capo Press books are available at special discounts for bulk purchases in the U.S. by corporations, institutions, and other organizations. For more information, please contact the Special Markets Department at the Perseus Books Group, 11 Cambridge Center, Cambridge, MA 02142, or call (800) 255-1514 or (617) 252-5298, or e-mail special.markets@perseusbooks.com.

2 3 4 5 6 7 8 9—09 08 07 06 05

To the children and parents
who have taught us so much through the years

Contents

Contents

Acknowledgments

We would like to thank parents across the country for having first urged us to write these concise, accessible books on topics of the utmost importance to them, for without their vision they might never have been written. Thanks too go to Karin Ajmani, Marie Caldwell, Geoffrey Canada, Marilyn Joseph and the Baby College staff, Karen Lawson and her late husband Bart, David Saltzman and Caressa Singleton for their unwavering support for our work, and from whom we have learned so much. As always, we would again like to thank our editor, Merloyd Lawrence, for her wisdom and guidance. Finally, we wish to express our gratitude to our families, not only for their encouragement and patience but also for the lessons they have taught us that we have sought to impart in this book.

Preface

Ever since I wrote the first *Touchpoints* book, published in 1992, I have been asked by parents and professionals all over the country to write some short, practical books on the common challenges that parents face as they raise their children. Among the most common are crying, discipline, sleep, toilet training, feeding, sibling rivalry, and aggression.

In my years of pediatric practice, families have taught me that problems in these areas often arise predictably as a child develops. In these short books I have tried to address the problems that parents are bound to encounter as their children regress just before they make their next developmental leap. Each book describes these "touchpoints"—of crying, discipline, sleep, toilet training, feeding, sibling rivalry, and aggression—so that parents can better understand their child's behavior. Each also offers specific suggestions as to how parents can help their child master the challenges they face in these areas so that they can get back on track.

In general, these books focus on the challenges of the first six years of life, though occasionally older children's issues are referred to. In the final section, special problems are discussed, though these short books are not intended to cover these topics exhaustively. Instead, we hope that these books will serve as easy-to-use guides for parents to turn to as they face their child's growing pains, or "touchpoints" that signal exciting leaps of development.

As with *Touchpoints Three to Six,* I have invited Joshua Sparrow, M.D., to co-author these books with me, to add his perspective as a child psychiatrist. Though difficulties such as siblings who fight, compete, or won't share, for example, are both common and predictable, they make great demands on parents. These kinds of problems are for the most part temporary and not serious, yet without support and understanding, they can overwhelm a family, and send a child's development seriously off course. It is our hope that the straightforward information provided in these books will help prevent those unnecessary derailments, and provide reassurance for parents in times of uncertainty, so that the excitement and joy of helping a young child grow can be rekindled.

UNDERSTANDING
SIBLING RIVALRY
The
Brazelton Way

CHAPTER 1

Sibling Relationships

"Guess what! I'm pregnant with my second child," mothers tell me, and then proceed to break into tears. "Are you worried that you'll desert the older child?" I ask. Fighting back more tears, they swear they'll never do that. But they know they will, as soon as the new baby arrives, and I know they will, too.

"No parent ever feels that she has enough mothering to go around," Erik Erikson once said to me. "When one child needs her, she feels she is ignoring the other. Then, when both need her, she feels she hasn't been able to satisfy either of them." She must protect the baby, but to do this, she must often hold off the older child. The feeling that you are deserting one for the other can be crushing. Early on, parents resolve to treat each child fairly, but also begin worrying about how they'll ever manage to be fair to both. Parents wonder, "How will I be able to see both children's sides at once?" They fret about the inevitable rivalry between siblings, and they may not realize that each child will learn to adapt to the other, and that both children will learn to share their parents with each other.

In our mainstream culture, parents' attention to children's individual needs has become more important than valuing their ability to share and learn to live together. In some families, parents who value individual accomplishment more than the strength of the family encourage competition among siblings. Yet these same parents still want to know: "How will I get rid of the rivalry between my children?" Even when they seem to be raising each child to put his or her own goals before the family's, parents ask: "How can I help my children learn to care about each other?" Ask any parents about their hopes for their children's relationships, and you'll hear, "I want them to care about each other, and to look after each other—for the rest of their lives." Even in this competitive culture, parents believe that their children are their "brother's keepers." Our own children call each other before they call us when they have a problem. We are proud of that.

It is our hope that this book will help parents reach this important goal for their children. To some extent, sibling relationships are out of parents' hands. But parents can make choices as they respond to each child and to the squabbles that can influence these relationships, for better or for worse. They can help turn their children's interactions, negative and positive, into rich and valuable opportunities to learn about each other and how to live together. They can foster strong relationships among siblings by avoiding bids to take sides, and by resisting temptations to enlist one child as a parent's ally against a sibling. Parents should expect that each child will have to learn how the other functions, and how to make himself or herself understood.

When I was making films about child development, a mother brought her 5-month-old baby to "perform" for us. The baby would laugh on cue, she'd hold up one hand, she'd sit and try to crawl. She was amazing. "How has she learned so much?" I asked. The mother pointed to the baby's 6-year-old brother, who was carrying out all our commands across the room from her. As he did so, this baby would imitate him almost precisely. Each time she performed, he would grin and wave at her. No other reward but his approval.

Competitive feelings may fuel these learning processes, but learning to live together with others is, of course, the larger goal. Parents may feel that when a new baby arrives, they have deserted the previous one. But each sibling is a gift to the others.

Beyond Rivalry—Learning from Siblings

Is there an advantage in having siblings? I think so. In the 1980s, I was sent to Beijing by UNICEF, along with a group from the Society for Research in Child Development, to study the one-child family. We compared 4- and 5-year-olds from one-child families and two-child families. The preschoolers were scored on several items:

1. Did they share toys easily?
2. Did they think of others or of themselves first?
3. Did other children like them?
4. Did they appear to be self-centered in their play?

Children from one-child families scored lower on all items. Raised without other children by six adults (grandparents and parents) who cater to them, these only children were not learning to share with others, nor did they enjoy giving to others. Of course, the qualities of sharing and giving can be encouraged in only children when parents are aware that they'll need to make a special effort. If parents recognize the child's need to be with other children and to be taught to share, there can be advantages to being an only child; for example, an only child is always sure of her place in the family.

Children from families with more than one child must learn to share. Siblings learn from each other about how to recognize each others' needs and to balance them with their own. Through their tiresome squabbles, they teach each other to negotiate and to compromise, and to include each other in their decision making. Every parent hopes that they'll also learn to care about each other. An only child will need to turn to cousins and close friends for these experiences.

As siblings learn from each other, and to adapt to each other, rivalry and caring for the other become two sides of the same coin. As one develops, so will the other. I see sibling rivalry as an important way for each child to get to know the other: "How far can I go? How far can she? How far can I push her? What happens when she falls apart? What does it feel like to have her look up to me or to be furious at me?"

Watch the intense dedication of a small child to her older sibling's activities.* She watches, watches, watches. Then she imitates every move he makes, in exactly the same order—all at once. An impressive feat! If you were able to enter her mind, you might see her brain register the entire sequence before she performs it. In the more usual learning of a behavior, without a sibling model, that same child would more likely try to break down the sequence and practice pieces of it, only putting them together after mastering each step separately. Much more costly. Instead, though, a small child can learn in hunks from imitation and identification with an older sibling. Imagine the rapt devotion that this way of learning demands! The younger child almost *absorbs* a part of the older one. Think what an advantage it can be to have an older sibling to learn from. She knows intimately how he works, what makes him tick. Even without demonstrating it, she incorporates his style and his excitement as part of her own.

---

*Throughout this chapter and the next, we refer to the younger sibling as "she," and to the older one as "he," except in discussions involving gender differences.

After a period of such intense admiration and imitation, the younger child may have had enough. She may become overwhelmed and exhausted. What does she do? She sets off a minor explosion—tearing down his block tower, interfering with his game, climbing into his lap, obstructing his view of his toys. She'll use ingenious techniques to wreck what he's doing when she knows she's not yet able to copy it herself and win back his attention.

She's trying to divert him from his own play to nurture her at a time when she might otherwise have a meltdown. Of course, he will react by resenting her and turning on her. A parent will hear her scream, rush in to protect her, and reprimand the older child for being jealous and insensitive toward his younger sister! A typical case of sibling rivalry involving conflict as well as learning.

What has the older sibling learned? As he played, he was aware of his sister's studied interest. He felt rewarded by her entranced observation. He carefully geared his own activity down to a level that she could imitate. As she imitated him, he made his movements more complex, leading her slowly and carefully up to another level. As he added each step, he used his peripheral vision to see how far she could follow. He felt proud as he learned to nurture, teach, and lead. But when he led her too far, she collapsed. He had not learned her limits. Or had he?

Her failure to keep up may have bothered him more than her teasing and meltdown. Disappointed, he reacted to her with his own loss of control. Meanwhile, he'd learned, from her intense identification with him, how to adapt to her differences. The screaming and fighting distracted the parents from seeing the learning occurring through the siblings' interaction. For the children, too, rivalry can cover up other intense feelings about each other.

Ghosts from the Nursery

Sibling conflict is likely to call up old feelings, and powerful ones, in parents. They're bound to relive childhood experiences with their own siblings. The child expert Selma Fraiberg called these "ghosts from the nursery." When parents are aware of how much old memories can influence their reactions to their children, they may find that they are better able to choose their response.

"My older brother was always mean to me," one parent recalled, explaining her overreaction to her oldest son's pestering of the younger one. The traumatic aspects of the past are often more readily remembered than the more positive ones; as a result, parents may miss out on the positive aspects of their own children's struggles. They'll be mobilized, of course, by the younger child's cry for help, and by the older child's out-of-control behavior. Meanwhile, they may be ignoring the older brother's tenderness and caretaking at certain points in these conflicts. Instead, they may remember their own pasts: "He seemed to care, then he deserted me and let me down." Yet positive aspects of a parent's own sibling experiences can serve as a guide. Try sharing both sides with your family. Then you'll be more aware of your biases!

Bringing a second child into the family is a lot more challenging than any parent wants to admit. It's not simply a matter of adding another soul to the teetering balance of a family. It disrupts all the old relationships, and it requires a new and more complicated equation. The new baby is not at the same stage of development, and may not have the same temperament as the older one to whom you have adjusted. Having two children involves a lot more than having one plus one!

When siblings tear at each other, parents want to protect the baby, but at the same time feel that they are ignoring the older child. They might react by trying to be fair. They try to sort out the sequence, the reason for the younger child's misery. But they'll never know exactly what happened. As they react, ignoring or punishing the older one for "being mean," they are painfully aware that they are not playing fair.

Can parents learn from these feelings? Can they learn that rarely will they really know what started a sibling struggle, or which child was guilty and which one was innocent? Often, they'll both be both. Parents will need to comfort both children for their disappointment in having broken the exciting bubble of play and learning about each other, and having fallen back into bickering and squeals.

A parent can use a lap to gather them both up, and then say, "You care so much about each other. You are learning so much about each other. Of course, you're both miserable when you can't get along. I can understand that. Can you? When you can stop fighting, you can play with each other again. Or you can leave each other to play alone. It's your decision." In the midst of an outburst, of course, this is easier said than done.

To handle such a crisis, parents will need to:

1. Calm their own feelings;
2. Gather up the squirming fighting children;
3. Sit down;
4. Encourage each child to stop blaming the other and to take responsibility for his or her own role in learning to get along.

This approach is not learned overnight, but it can be a goal. And in the process, parents and children learn to be a family.

Temperament: Sibling Differences

As siblings learn to get along, they'll have to deal with their differences in temperament. For example, on the surface, a quiet, sensitive child may not appear to react to her brother's boisterous taunts and jeers. She seems to wait to be attacked. Her behavior is so submissive that an observer wants to tell her, "Don't let him take advantage of you like that." Her focus seems to be directed inward. Her breathing changes, but she does not move. As he descends on her to tease her, she watches him. She listens but doesn't seem to respond. She has already learned to be as still as possible, to avoid becoming his target. When her brother builds up to a crescendo of activity, she might become even quieter, and more watchful. As he tears around the room, her only move is to place herself in his path. They collide, but she resorts only to silent sobs, her body limp and unresponsive. A parent's reaction will be to rush to comfort her, while her brother stands by, shrouded in guilt and misery.

Over time, a younger sibling may even take on the behavior of a victim. In school, other children begin to respond to her passive withdrawal. She may become the victim of bullying, or be excluded as a result. Parents will wish that she would react more openly and fight back. But the style of a child like this is quiet observation and compliance.

If the first child is a highly active handful, parents may ask about the second, "Do you suppose she knew I couldn't stand another one like that?" If they feel responsible for her gentle ways, parents may try to change her. But they'll do best if they make sure she knows she's accepted just as she is. Then they can watch carefully for their tendency to reward and reinforce her passivity and leave more room for her to stand up for herself.

Slotting

Often, almost magically, children fit themselves into slots in a family, different from each other, as if they "needed" to take special roles. A child with a quiet temperament who has a sibling full of hard-driving intensity may be led straight into an even more withdrawn role.

Parents can see this kind of reaction as one way that children learn about each other, and each others' temperament. A child's passivity could be attributed partly to the effect of temperament, including hypersensitivity to sound, to touch, or to being approached. But parents need also to recognize that their reactions reinforce children further in these various slots.

Parents can learn a lot by watching two siblings, while keeping out of sight. To their surprise, they may find that a boisterous older sibling likes to play with the quiet one as well as to tease her. When they sit on the floor together, he'll slow down, build a block tower for her, watch her eyes grow large and glisten. In her own way, a watchful sibling pushes an active one to new mastery.

An adoring younger sibling learns that the older one will come to her when she calls. When they build up to a crisis, a word from her may avert it. She will begin to realize that she can woo him and win occasionally; parents will observe that children save these touching moments for times when they are alone. Free of others' reactions, each child expands his range beyond his "slot."

Think how much children learn by adapting to each other's temperament. They can learn to share, to give, to console, to care about each other. Each also experiences the deeper satisfaction that such gestures bring.

Siblings: A Parent's Presence

Sibling rivalry is much more likely to build up to a crescendo if a parent is nearby. I've never heard of a sibling who has really hurt another unless a parent was close at hand. I'm sure it has happened, but I suspect that it is rare. A major aim of siblings' rivalry is to draw in a parent. Siblings want a parent involved to heighten the excitement, but also to be sure the parent is there to limit the danger of losing control. The assurance that a parent is nearby sets a boundary on how far the rivalry can be taken. It is almost as if children set up their struggles when a parent is near to be certain that they will be helped to learn how to stop themselves.

A wise parent will see sibling clashes as an opportunity for learning. But you will first need to handle your own angry and protective reactions. Then, you can gather up each child. Sit down with them both. Calmly face the episode together and with as little blame as possible. To an active older child, you might say, "You could have hurt her. I doubt that you'd feel good about that." To a quiet but provocative younger one: "Your teasing made him angry. That may be why he got after you." And to both: "You need to take care of this yourselves. But until you can stop hurting each other, I'll have to stop you. Let me know when you feel ready to play together again—without clobbering each other!" You'll be giving them the chance to learn to take care of each other, your long-term goal.

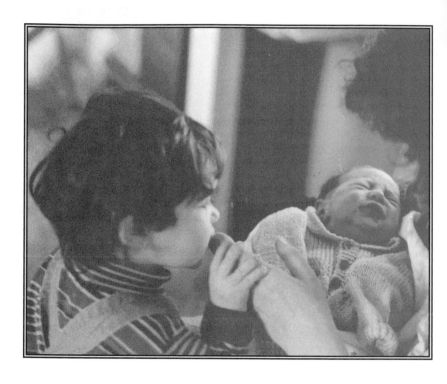

CHAPTER 2

Touchpoints of Sibling Rivalry

Touchpoints are the expectable times in a child's development when he slips backward to gather steam for the next step ahead. During these short periods of regression, parents and siblings can't help but react to the child's upsetting behavior. As the child regresses, the whole family is bound to fall apart. I call these periods "touchpoints" because I have found that if I can "touch" into the parent-child system at such a time, I can help the family reorganize. Each touchpoint places stress on developing sibling relationships, but it can also be an opportunity for each to learn about the other, and to care more deeply. In this chapter, we'll look at the opportunities for siblings to learn about each other and discover how to get along together as they grow.

Each child will be challenged as he faces the other's new skills or fears, and his own. These touchpoints are inevitable and healthy steps toward a child's optimal development. To illustrate these challenges and opportunities, we will describe the touchpoints of an older brother and a younger sister, about 3 years apart. Each section of this chapter is titled to reflect the younger sibling's age at each touchpoint. We've also tried to note how these touchpoints might unfold somewhat differently for children of different genders, or with a larger or smaller age gap between them.

The Prenatal Touchpoint

Facing a second pregnancy is both thrilling and daunting. Parents will ask themselves: "Was I right to get pregnant? What will this do to my older child? Can I manage with two? How could I ever love another child as much?" When sibling rivalry arises, they are bound to feel responsible, and guilty.

Later, they will find they need not divide their love, for they will love each child *differently.* But before the new baby arrives to help parents make this discovery, they may feel they must try not to grow attached to the new one, but instead must focus even more on the one they already have. The fear of "deserting" the older child is inevitable.

All parents wish they could eliminate the older child's negative reactions to the new baby: "How can we make him *want* a little brother or sister?" This parental pressure makes the older child feel unacceptable as he is, and wonder if he really deserves to be replaced. Of course he knows that he both does and doesn't want a new sibling.

If he's in childcare, parents will also worry: "Will the teacher help protect my first child from this blow?" If the firstborn child is not yet in childcare, this would be a difficult time for him to begin. Parents' ambivalent feelings about the pregnancy often lie just beneath the surface of concerns like this. Although these feelings are most prominent with the second pregnancy, they are likely to be present with any subsequent pregnancy. It can be a challenge to see each new baby as a "gift" to the family.

But parents needn't feel that it is their role to protect their children from all the feelings—anger, jealousy, and others— that they will experience with a new baby. All these feelings are inevitable, not only with new siblings but throughout life. Adjusting to a new sibling is a child's opportunity to learn about these feelings and how to handle them. And parents *can* help.

With each subsequent pregnancy, I felt that my wife and I were pushing our luck. We had a perfect child. How could the next one live up to her? If the one-to-be couldn't, how would we nurture unequal children? All the fears of the first pregnancy are relived, but with a new dimension, never dreamed of the first time around: "What will it mean to the older one if this baby has problems? How could I impose this risk on the child I already have?"

Parents need to face their own questions before they begin to help the first child handle his reactions to the new baby. Parents are bound to remember times from their own childhood when their parents couldn't spare enough for them, when a sibling was cuddled and fussed over, and when they were "ignored." This kind of identification with their older child will help parents to understand him. Yet, it won't do, of course, for you to present the new baby as a big mistake or a bad dream, even though you are giving permission to the older child to voice these and other feelings.

When Do I Tell My First Child?

You never don't tell him. As soon as you know a new baby is on the way, it can be discussed in the family openly. Your discussion is not so much an announcement as an acceptance of the baby as a future step for the whole family. But try not to overdo the information. Too much discussion of the wonder of it all will set him up for even more rivalry with the "thing" in Mommy's tummy.

One couple told me that they had discussed the baby-to-be so much and so often that the older child was sick of it by the seventh month. He was tired of being prepared for so long. Talking about the new baby coming into the family in an accepting way is different from excitedly preparing the older child for a major event. Parents can make it clear the family will "all deal with it together" without dramatizing that "everything will be different and you will have a big adjustment to make."

Why Shouldn't We Wait Until He Knows I'm Pregnant?   He may know almost as soon as you do. Early in the pregnancy, a mother's moods will change. Both parents will catch themselves being dreamily remote, or stressed. Even before a mother's belly has expanded, she may find that plopping down on the floor to play isn't the same as it used to be. Even a young child will notice.

I remember Leslie. Leslie was two and a half and came to my office for a checkup. He was a handsome curly headed, dark-skinned toddler—the adored child of his lovely parents. Every time he leaned over in my office, every time he'd lower himself to the floor, he'd let out a soft grunt. I thought that he might be hiding a bellyache or some problem in his joints. I felt his stomach more carefully. No tenderness. I examined his hips and legs. No problem. I watched him walk. Absolutely perfect, even graceful. I kept observing him. Each grunting sound made me more alert and more anxious. No physical signs. Finally, out of the blue, I questioned his mother: "Are you pregnant?" "No," she assured me. A few days later, she called me to say, "I *am* pregnant. But I'm only eight weeks along. How did you know before I did?" I was quick to answer: "I didn't, really. But Leslie did." Leslie knew his mother had changed before even she realized she was pregnant.

The job for parents is to give a name to the change the child senses, and gradually to make it seem real to the child. You might tell him, "You and Mommy and Daddy are going to have a baby. You can help us with the baby. You'll be a big *brother.*" Then, listen. Don't keep telling him about the new baby. Wait for his questions. They'll come.

When he passes a baby carriage, watch his eyes and his behavior change. If you can be quietly patient, he may say, "Like that?"

"Uh-huh."

"Can I help push the carriage?"

"Of course. You can be my best helper."

He is already learning about giving. You are helping him discover its rewards. This is, of course, one of the most important lessons a sibling can ever learn.

Shouldn't We Keep It to Ourselves for As Long As We Can, Just in Case Something Goes Wrong? I don't think so. If you do lose the baby, your child will know that something has happened. You cannot and should not try to hide your sadness. He will be far more troubled by such a tragedy if he has to guess at why your face and eyes look so different now, why your movements have become slow and heavy, why you have become so silent. He won't be as sad about the loss as you are, and he might learn to comfort you. As you share your sorrow with him, he'll learn how to share feelings with others, including, later on, his siblings. (See *Miscarriages* in Chapter Three.)

How Can I Help My Child Understand What Is Really Going on Inside? As a mother's belly increases in size, and as she becomes less agile, she may want to let the child feel the movements of the fetus. We used to feel our last unborn baby's movements. My wife would lie on the couch to keep her feet up; then our three little girls and I would put our hands where we could feel their little brother-to-be moving.

Toward the end of the pregnancy, we listened to the heartbeat with my stethoscope. (The heartbeat is not always easy to find. Parents should search for it first if they want to invite a child to listen to it.) When they had detected the rhythm, we'd clap our hands to make a loud noise. The baby's heartbeat would change. Or we'd turn off the light, and then suddenly turn it on again. The baby's heart rate would respond. Parents who witness such fetal behavior like to see this as early preparation for noisy siblings. The girls would shout with glee: "He sees! He hears!" When the baby moved, they were ecstatic. Before he was born, we were already sharing him as a person.

If your older child has a friend who already has another baby in the family, this friend might be able to share the reality of a newborn. It can be a rehearsal, a chance to practice, if it's kept low key.

How Will My Toddler React? Later in the pregnancy, toddlers often begin to walk with a wide-based gait, their knees bowed and bellies out in front of them, as if they were identifying with their pregnant mothers. Eating "to get fat like Mommy" and even withholding bowel movements are common signs of the child's attempt to be like his mother. These reactions and imitations are a child's way of trying to understand the change in the family that is coming. By identifying with Mommy, with her swelling "stomach" and her awkward walk, the child is already facing the intrusion and readying himself for a new role and new relationships.

Meanwhile, everyone is talking about the changes that will occur. Of course, an older sibling has his questions: "When?" "Why?" (Aren't I good enough?) "Will he be like me? Who will take care of me?" All these questions deserve answers. As you answer, you'll demonstrate your caring, and help your child "become a big brother." But information that is over his head won't help. Try to adjust your answers to his level of understanding (for this, consult Brazelton and Sparrow, *Touchpoints Three to Six,* listed in the *Bibliography*). What you say may not matter as much as your being available. Your responsiveness is most important. This is a good time for each parent to start planning a regular "date" with the older child. Talk about it all week: "You and I will have our time together later this week. You can ask me all your questions and we can be together by ourselves. You are my big boy now and you'll always be my first love."

On one of these excursions, your child may ask you, "How did the baby get inside your tummy?" This is a question to be prepared for. We recommend that you answer truthfully, with information simplified to suit the child's age and ability to understand. If you offer a fantasy about a stork, or magic that is later contradicted by a worldly peer, you will have made yourself an unreliable authority.

Why not simply say, "Daddy puts his penis [make sure your child knows what that is] inside Mommy's vagina [your child will need to know what that is, too]. Little seeds come out of Daddy's penis to make an egg inside Mommy's vagina [it's the uterus, actually, but keep it simple for now] ready to become a baby!" Certainly, very young children will shake their heads with bewilderment, and slightly older ones with disbelief. By five and six, they are most likely to be disgusted. One six-year-old exclaimed, "But what if Daddy goes pee?"

You may feel queasy, but wouldn't you rather have your child face all this with you than with an only slightly more informed child? Children usually don't pay much attention to words they aren't ready for or don't understand. Watch your child's face, and stop when it is clear he's heard enough. The main goal is to show him your willingness to answer. (See the books listed in the bibliography for more help with this topic.)

Labor and Delivery and the Older Child

As the delivery approaches, talk about going to the hospital to help the baby come "out." Let your child know exactly who will stay with him at home, and who will take him to visit his mother and the new baby at the hospital. You can even drive by the hospital beforehand to show him where they'll be. It is a wonderful time for a father or a grandparent to point out that he or she will be there for the older child. One of the most rewarding experiences for me as a father was the opportunity to be completely available for my older daughters—and to have them all to myself! If a less familiar sitter will be with your child, let him get to know the caregiver ahead of time. This is no time for him to worry that he might be handed off to a stranger. That fear might be part of his fantasy about the new baby anyway.

Toward the end, be ready for the older child to build up excitement as does the rest of the family. Tantrums, whining, sleep setbacks, food refusal, and bedwetting can all be expected. These will arise from his confusion about all the intense anticipation as well as from his awareness of your heightened vulnerability. You will be exhausted and physically stressed yourself; but remember, he is working to adjust. The more he does now to share his distress, the easier it may be for him later. He may also start to cling, as if to protest the coming separation. Of course, this will hit home for you. He'll sense your sadness at having to leave him. He's liable to play on whatever guilty feelings you may have.

When labor begins, and you must leave for the hospital, be sure to say goodbye. Trying to skip out unnoticed may seem easier, but it can leave him more frightened. Tell him again that you're going to the hospital for a few days. Remind him that he can call you, and come to visit. Reassure him again about who will be with him. Tell him when you expect to come home. Show him on the calendar. All this preparation leaves him with a known structure and expectation. A mother might even want to make a videotape of herself as she reads him his favorite bedtime story. His father or grandparent can play it for him on the nights she's away. This can protect him from his deepest fear—that she's "gone off to have the baby" and leave him. This fear is predictable for a young child, but parents can help allay it.

Reclaiming the Crib, and the "Big Boy's Bed." When parents are expecting a second child, they are often tempted to reclaim the first child's crib to ready it for the new baby. Don't. If the older child is still in the crib during the pregnancy, don't make him move unless you absolutely have to (for example, if he weighs too much for the crib, or is climbing out and at risk of being hurt). He's already feeling displaced, and he will only feel more so once the baby is here. Instead, you'll have to get another crib for the baby and then wait until the older child really feels proud of being a *big* brother. You may be ready before he is to see him this way. But you'll have to wait.

Pushing him too far, too soon, is only likely to end in one regression or another. Bedwetting might be an understandable result of an unwanted switch in sleeping arrangements. A big bed can feel way too big, and he will miss the reassuring crib rails that seem to say, "This is where you belong." Without them, your child may regress in another way—waking up in the middle of the night to wander out of his "big boy bed" to see whether he can find some special time alone with you.

The New Baby

Although you may have prepared the older child over and over for a baby, he is likely to have imagined a new playmate—someone his own age, not a tiny, fragile, red-faced screamer or a boring little ball of blankets that sleeps all the time. Be prepared for his disappointment. This may be hard to put up with, given all the trouble you've just gone through, your own excitement, and your exhaustion.

In the Hospital

Your older child may race over to the bassinet, or barely dare to approach. But, either way, don't expect him to be interested in the baby for more than a moment when he comes to the hospital to see you both. Quickly, he'll lose interest and try to persuade you to interact with him. In these first moments, try to make him the center of your attention. If you and your older child have talked or sung to the baby before she was born, you can invite him to test out the new baby's reactions now that she is here: "See how she turns to *your* voice. She remembers your talking to her before she came out of Mummy's tummy. Now, you're her big brother."

If you need to feed her or change her, let him assist. You can look for small ways that he can safely help. He may feel so proud to offer a diaper or hold a bottle. If you breastfeed her when he's around, be prepared for him to want to try it himself. He won't be able to, of course, and will quickly lose interest. But he'll treasure the cuddling. "You're our big boy now. You are so special."

When he's in the hospital with the new baby, the older child may be either quiet or overwhelmed, or he may be frightened and out of control. If he's overwhelmed, be prepared for him to ignore you and to withdraw, as if your attempts to reach him were painful. Or he may be excited and overactive. If there are others in the room, he may show off. Or he may suddenly collapse into a tantrum.

Don't be surprised if he wants to ignore the new baby, or if he's angry with you. Don't take his rejecting behavior too personally. Try to help him through it so that he can return to his close relationship with you. Try to entice him to cuddle in your lap, or talk with him about how much you have missed him. If he melts down, soothe him and help him soothe himself. He'll need your help in understanding his own reactions. "It was scary when Mommy had to go to the hospital. And now everyone's making such a fuss over this new baby."

Falling in Love—Again
Meanwhile, you are falling in love with the new baby. Your earlier worries about "deserting" your first child for the second quickly give way to these new feelings. The baby is so winning, so deliciously dependent. Still, any new parent of a second child will be concerned about the first child's adjustment. Being away from the older child—perhaps for the first time—is bound to be a heightened situation for you and him.

It may surprise you as parents to find that you feel so enamored of the newborn, and so let down when the older child isn't ready to take a more grownup role. Instead, he's likely to backslide again—with more fussing, trouble falling asleep or separating, and other old behaviors of the past. Remember that these temporary setbacks can help him prepare to take on his new "older brother" role.

But this is not the time to expect a mature reaction, or even to wish for it. Not yet. He has sensed the crisis of the birth and delivery, and of his changing relationship with you. Your time away from home to deliver the infant makes this separation explicit. He knows now that the baby has taken away his old role in the family. Is he already trying to figure out the new part he'll have to play?

Going Home

When you arrive home, I'd suggest that you have a new and special toy ready to give your older child. Preferably a baby of his own. One that he can feed and diaper while you are changing yours. (You may want to buy him one before the baby is born, but save it for when you all come home.) If he's more interested in trucks, give him one he can fuel, wash, and "nurture" while you care for your baby. This is a chance for him to model on your nurturing.

Don't be afraid to set limits on how much he can handle the new baby. Limits will be reassuring for him as his feelings about her come to the surface. If he wants to hold her "like you do," ask him to sit down in a chair. You will need to stay right by his side. Then, he can learn to put one hand under her neck and head to protect her. He can learn to cuddle her, to give her a water bottle. He can begin to learn how to help diaper her and to talk to her as he does so. He will be learning how to "be a big brother." With you right nearby.

If the older child soon loses interest in being a big brother, don't be surprised, and don't make too much of it. Though he

How to Help an Older Child
Adjust to a Brand-New Baby

- Let the older child know how much you've missed him.
- Let him know that the baby has been added to the family and is not a replacement: "Now you have a brand new baby sister. But nobody could ever be just like you!"
- Hold him close, and remind him of experiences you've shared and will share again.
- Understand and be ready for his need to fall back on old behavior you'd thought he'd outgrown. Don't expect too much of him right now.
- If he pushes you to discipline him, remember that limits can be especially reassuring to him with the new baby around. Limits mean to him that his parents "haven't changed, still love me, and will stop me when I need it."
- Don't urge him to be "such a good big brother." This job won't always seem so appealing. It will mean more when he finds his own motivation to fill the role.
- Guard against wanting him to grow up! He will, when he's ready. And his younger sibling is already pushing him enough.

may at times be proud of his new role, it'll be a burden for him, too. Expect him, instead, to want to be your baby again. Let him.

Many children who are just discovering what it means to be an older sibling begin to be cruel to the dog or cat. Stop your child firmly, but gently, and let him know that you can't allow this. Help him with his feelings by letting him know that his anger is understandable even though he can't take it out on the pet. It won't help if these feelings are allowed to go underground.

An older child is likely to feel that the new baby has displaced him because he was not "good enough," or even "bad." A 3- or 4-year-old can often recall mischief that made you angry and made you, in his mind, want to replace him. He is bound to feel that if he could have been all that you wanted, you'd not have needed a new baby.

A child who is older, 6 or 7 years old or more, may just ignore the baby—and you. He may even seem to disappear because he's spending more time with his friends, or dawdling on his way home from school. Instead of being your companion as you get to know the baby, he seems to want to avoid you—to punish you. Time alone with you and your willingness to listen and answer questions will be all the more important.

The First Months at Home

The new baby's demands will increase—more frequent feedings, fussing at the end of the day—but a mother's energy may not yet have returned. She may well be depressed at first, or in a few more weeks. Whether she is or not, the older child senses her exhaustion. Yet his demands increase, too. It's almost as if he must test to be sure that she'll recover, that she can still care for him despite her fatigue. Teasing and testing, refusing bedtime and waking up each time the baby does—all are to be expected.

Tantrums and Testing

Tantrums become more common, especially when the new baby is being fed and at other inconvenient times. Parents can try to anticipate times such as these when the baby needs their attention, and when the older child will want it, too. When they can be predicted in advance, and if there's time, try attending to the older child first. You might even use this time to help him start a game or project that he can continue while you are caring for the baby, one that he can proudly show you when you and he are both finished.

When you have to feed the baby, the older child might be able to play beside you so that you can comment on what he's doing from time to time. If the baby falls off to sleep after nursing, you may have a little time with the older child for cuddling, rocking, reading, singing, or just chatting. You'll feel as though you never have a chance to catch your breath!

When you pick up the baby, you might say, "Go get your baby and let's all feed together. Watch how the baby quiets down when she starts sucking. Does yours? Can you imitate her?" Help the older child feel that he can participate in caring for the new baby instead of feeling left out. He can set up his own regular rituals—with the baby, or with his baby doll—that help him to feel included.

Let him climb into your lap next to the baby, even to hug her. If you are breastfeeding, let him try out your milk from the other breast if he wants to. He's not likely to try it more than twice—unless he's not yet been weaned himself. Expect times when he tires of the cozy triangle. His natural buoyancy, his need to establish himself and his independence will return. Slithering off your lap and away from the baby, he'll say, "Thass 'nuf, Mom! Come play with me!" He'll try to drag you away from the feeding. You'll resist and grow irritated as his antics interrupt the baby's sucking. A toddler may build up to a tantrum. He may make it dramatic enough to send the baby into a startle and a squeal. Your blood pressure will rise. Your anger will surface: "I've done all I can. Now leave us alone."

If his tantrum escalates and he lies on the floor kicking and screaming, you'll hear a plaintive note in his voice; this is his way of letting you know how deserted he feels. You are caught—and feel split in two. Where is your duty as a parent? What can you do? You'll have to say, "I'm right here. But I can't come to you. When you calm down, we'll sit together in our rocking chair as soon as I can. Then we can read your favorite story. But first you'll have to calm down, and wait." WAIT? What a terrible word for a toddler to hear!

Watch him master his distress. As the tantrum subsides, he'll put his thumb in his mouth, and his eyes will grow large and soft and anguished. He'll roll over on his side, away from you, sucking vigorously and whimpering loudly. You will feel his hurt and loneliness. For a moment, you may even feel like rushing the new baby into her crib to go to him. Wait!

He'll gradually stop his moaning. Slowly, he'll pull himself together—to get up and seek out some forbidden activity that he knows you will react to. He'll pull you away from the baby more successfully by his "badness." He'll show you that he is "bad," that you did need a new baby, a quiet and docile one. In his play, he'll act out his fear of why he "lost" you.

What do you do? Must you shape his "bad" behavior into "good?" Can you? Not very likely. But you can set limits on it, and help him learn from that process. When he tests you, you might say, "Put that vase back on the table. I told you I'd come in a minute."

When he keeps up the testing, go to him with the baby in your arms, or when she's safely in her crib. As you start up, he may do what you've asked. If he doesn't, take the vase from him and put it out of his reach. Then try saying, for example, "I know you want to play. But that's not how to ask me. Get me a diaper for the baby and then we'll have time to play." Sheepishly, he goes for a diaper, perhaps scattering the whole stack. But you've helped him learn the limit. By your commitment to teaching him better ways to behave, you've shown him that he is not a "bad boy."

These blow-ups are rare at first, so you'll have a chance to figure out how to help him with them. Later, they may become more frequent, and you'll feel besieged. His wearisome behavior will leave you feeling even more cut off from him. You'll feel angry as he pulls you into battles to draw you to him. You'd like to have enough energy to take care of him, but it just may not be there. If you feel depressed, this will drain your resources for him. Cuddling for a moment, while the baby is asleep, is one way to care for him that you may still have energy for.

End-of-the-Day Fussing

The new baby's fussy period every evening, which predictably begins by the end of the first month and is over by the start of the fourth month, is difficult for everyone. When parents try everything to comfort the baby, the older child senses their desperation. At times, he falls apart, too; at others, he plays a comforting role. He climbs into his parents' laps. He strokes his mother's cheeks when she seems overwhelmed. Sometimes, his meltdowns seem less passionate. At others, he seems to compete with his sister by screeching more loudly than ever. She'll stop to listen to him briefly.

When the baby begins to smile and coo, he watches his parents very seriously as they work to attract her attention. At about 8 weeks, she seems to brighten up for him, too. When he leans over her, calling out "Bay-beeee, bay-beeee" and nodding to her, she'll smile and gurgle at him. His parents openly approve and they laugh together at the baby's antics. It is all so exciting that he may take her toes in his mouth and suck on them.

But expect surprises. As he grows excited, he might bite one of her toes. The baby will scream. His parents turn on him, and holler: "Don't you ever do that again." The magic moment disappears. The older child feels abandoned and guilty all over again, and doesn't understand why. Excitement causes buildups like this that are hard to control. This is a time for a father to sit down and comfort the older child while the mother fusses with the baby. Then he can explain to the child that he must learn to control himself. "I should have helped by breaking in sooner, before you got too excited to know when to stop."

Being a Big Boy and a Baby, Too

Although it may seem easy for an older child to take on the helping role of "big brother" or "big sister," don't be fooled. Along with pride in helping, and his discovery of his own "grownup-ness," he'll still resent the baby and feel sad about losing you. You can make it clear that there are times when he can help, and times when he can be a baby, too. The older child will be working so hard to understand the new baby, and to imitate her. He's telling you, "Why did you need her? I can do anything she can. I can still be your baby and please you." He is facing one of life's crises and learning how to cope with it, in the safety of your loving care.

Expect the older child to lose ground again at some point. Usually, it's in the area he's just mastered. If he's begun speaking, he may resort to "baby talk." If he's begun a new developmental step in any area—feeding himself, sleeping through the night, toilet mastery, conquering fears of strangers—expect a slide backwards. This is a touchpoint, a temporary falling apart that predicts a new step ahead. He is learning how to be a big brother.

Think what it means to the older child to have a two-month-old baby fuss every afternoon, and to have parents absorbed in worry over her. You can help him understand what's going on inside him. "Of course you want to talk like the baby, everyone pays

---

When You Must Discipline the Older Child, a Few Simple Steps Can Often Help

(See our book Discipline: The Brazelton Way, *listed in the* Bibliography.*)*

1. Stop him firmly but quietly.
2. Hold him, or use a time out if he's ready to comply.
3. If necessary, isolate him in his room.

Any or all of the above will break the cycle. Then:

1. Pick him up to hug and love him. "It's tough having a baby sister, isn't it? But I can't let you do that and you know it. I must be here to stop you—until you can stop yourself."
2. Watch his face and his eyes take it in—and soften.
3. After you've made contact with him and are feeling close again, let him help you with the baby. In that way, he'll begin to sense the goal of discipline, and to feel like a "big brother."

---

so much attention to her right now." Or, "Don't worry about wetting the bed. Once you get used to having a baby sister, it'll stop." Understanding will be far more effective than annoyance, or pressure to be a "big boy." These are bound to backfire into even more dramatic bids for you to let him be your baby again.

A Word of Caution
Many children seem to sail through these first months as if they were a breeze. They are compliant, even helpful. But don't ex-

pect it to last. The price of such a demanding new role may have to be paid at a later touchpoint in the older child's development, or in response to one of the baby's own touchpoints. Each of his steps backward is an opportunity for you and the child to learn together to master the next stage of development.

An older sibling who is 5 or 6 years old may not express his resentment and frustration through tantrums or meltdowns; instead, he may devise ways to attract your attention by spilling things, falling, needing your help with homework, and so on. Or he may come to your side as if to help, only to drag around and get sassy with you. But he needs the same understanding as a younger child. He will be better able to tell you how he feels than a younger child, and more able to help in a useful way once he feels understood.

6 Months

A Child's Play

Things have begun to go more smoothly. The older child seems to be finding outlets for his feelings. He is eager to meet a friend for a play date. Because your child's play may focus on feeding a baby, cuddling it, and singing to it, his play could at times bore the other child—unless he, too, has a baby in the family. But then your child is just as likely to throw the baby doll in a corner as he and his friend become super heroes, ready to rescue the next unsuspecting victim of evil. It is comforting to see that he can play out his feelings and turn to friends of his own age for comfort, and to continue on with his own growing up.

But at each new stage of a baby's development—crawling, the first steps, the first words—the older child feels left out and threatened all over again. Everyone who comes to see the family immediately gravitates to the baby. Even a more sensitive guest who purposely goes to the older child can't help but ask, "So what do you think about your baby sister?"

The older child may say, "I hate her," or lose interest in the guest at this point and run off. The older child's antics can be expected to become more frantic, more noisy, more intrusive. But they don't accomplish what the child wants. Instead, they just make everyone mad.

When the baby begins to reach for toys, the older child will hand her one, and then snatch it away. He'll quickly find out that he can torment her with this kind of teasing. When the older child attempts to "play" with the baby, his parents are likely to be pleased. But this is no time to leave it entirely to him. A baby's excitement and his own are bound to send the older child over the edge all too quickly.

When a baby first begins to sit up, an older child may seize on her shaky balance as a chance to topple her. "How could he!" parents who notice will gasp in horror. As the baby begins to creep, an older child is likely to step ever so close to her outstretched hands. It is as if the older child were threatened by the baby's advances, and he tries to fight them off before they encroach on his territory. Every parent should expect sibling battles when a baby starts moving around on her own.

The older child may innocently get down on the floor with the baby and entice her to crawl to him or to a toy. But as soon as she gets going, his motives become muddied. He may get on top of her as she crawls. If no one is looking, but parents are nearby, he might push her over. His parents will be shocked: "What a monster!" It is hard to want to comfort a child who behaves this way. And, yet, these antics are all evidence of his neediness, for comforting with limits.

When the baby begins to crawl, the older child is bound to fall apart. He may cry more easily now. He may cling to his mother and resist being left, even at a friend's house. If his father tries to persuade him to play games with the baby, he'll turn away from his father. He may not seem to be himself. Parents will have trouble hiding their disappointment. "You could help us with the baby instead of treating her like that. She's your sister and she adores you. She wants you to play with her. Why are you always angry with her?"

He may not know. A child of this age is likely to be flooded with feelings without knowing what they are. But if he can say, for example, "She takes my toys" or "She gets into my stuff," this is your chance to show him that you understand, and that of course you care about him, too. Try to hold back on your frustration with him. Don't expect him to understand the baby.

Instead, help him name and accept his feelings: "It's so annoying for you when she messes up what you are trying to do."

Then you can say, "You know she doesn't understand how important your projects are to you." He may not care about the reasons, but he will care that you've tried to understand him. If you can help him not to feel ashamed of his reactions to her, he'll be more likely to listen to you. To him this will mean that he isn't "so bad," and won't always have to behave in this way. When he needs your limits, he'll feel reassured by them.

Now it is even more important to make a special time for the older child. Ideally, each parent will have a time for him every day—without the baby. A time for rough housing or fantasy play right after supper, and, later, bedtime stories and the sharing of dreams. Or a little project during the baby's nap. At least plan a time at the end of the week when one of you can go off with the older child alone. Then, you can remind him about it the rest of the week. As he grows older, this time spent with him will become even more important. Single parents will want to find a reliable friend or relative to stay with the baby during special times away with the older child.

Parents' awareness of an older child's pain pushes them to face the conflicting feelings they themselves are bound to have. The desire to protect the baby is uppermost and need not be ignored. But the older child needs extra hugging and attention at each new exciting step in the baby's development. When he kneels down on the baby's level to imitate her, he is revealing his deep-seated feeling of having been replaced. But he can also be fascinated by the changes he sees in her. He is learning to understand and engage a much younger child, and to please his parents at the same time. He is learning to be a big brother. The baby's touchpoints are his, too.

The baby will now be entranced with him. When she hears his voice across the room, she sits up to listen. She will crawl to him, if he will stay in one place. Of course he won't! When he sees her creeping toward him, he changes places as if to trick her and lead her on. She is dogged. She keeps trying. He frustrates her and she learns to persevere. She watches him for a signal of approval as if he were her whole world. She isn't as vulnerable as she will be later to his provocations, his disdain, or his indifference. But don't expect him to be grateful for her devotion.

9 Months

If the older child's reaction to the new baby hasn't fully surfaced before, it is likely to when the baby reaches 9 months. The ability of the baby to move around, to get into the older child's toys is at a peak, and is not yet balanced by impulse control or judgment. "She just tore down my house," a 4-year-old might scream. "But you haven't played with it in a year!" "I don't care. It's mine!" He pushes the baby away, landing her on her back, leaving her screaming and paddling the air like an overturned turtle. "I'm glad. Now stay away," he scowls. He skulks away as if to hide from his feelings of guilt.

Parents may not see the guilty side, and they will be shocked by the pleasure he seems to take from having hurt his baby sibling. After rescuing the baby, you might say, for example, "I know it's hard to have a baby sister who's always wrecking your stuff. She really gets on your nerves, doesn't she?" When he knows that you understand his position too, you can add: "I can teach her not to touch your things, and so can you. But it's going to take a long time for her to learn. In the meantime, you know you mustn't push her like that. That's mean and you'll have to say you're sorry."

Finally, you might offer a suggestion: "When she heads over to you, hand her a toy you don't mind letting her use. Keep a bunch nearby. You know that anything you play with seems so special to her because she admires you so much!" Eventually, you may help this big brother see his little sister's annoying behavior as a sign of how important he is to her.

This is also the time to find a place where he can keep his favorite toys safe from her. Not that this strategy will settle everything, for it won't. He'll leave his toys out. She will get to them. They will each become enraged. Both children are learning how to bring each other to a peak of excitement. With a special place for the older child's toys, though, you can turn the job of protecting his belongings back to him.

A baby who has just learned to crawl will pick up fuzz, dirt, and particles off the floor. It will take extra vigilance to protect her. If the older child is old enough to have toys with small parts (at least 3 years old), he is likely to leave these easily swallowed and choked-on toy parts around. I would suggest that you keep these toys out of reach of both children. Take them out for the older child only when the baby's not around, or an adult can provide close supervision. (Clean-up will be easier, and you'll lose fewer pieces, too.) Ask the older child to help you pick up these tiny toy pieces when he's finished playing. But don't emphasize the baby's safety as the reason, or you could find that helping out will lose its charm for him.

Meanwhile, watch how proud your eldest can be of "his" baby. As she begins to perform in new ways, he will likely take pride in her new accomplishments. Parents may be thrown off by these seeming contradictions. But they illustrate the two sides of sibling rivalry: the fights, and the dedication.

As the baby tries to learn a new task, such as putting one block on top of another to build a tiny tower, the older child becomes an important model. Watch her sop him up. She'll imitate his movements almost exactly, almost in one piece. If her parent tried to show her the same task, she'd learn it one step at a time, not all at once.

An older sibling is so special as a model for a baby. He can almost pull her along in her development. When he frowns, she frowns. She will reproduce with great precision anything he does that she can imitate. Though his attention span is longer than hers, he will lose interest in her long before she does in him. A few months previously, she would forget about him as soon as he left her sight. But now, because she is able to think of him after he's deserted her ("object permanence"), she's bound to become more demanding, and to feel jilted whenever he stops playing with her.

12 Months

When the baby begins to stand, and then tries to let go and venture out, parents can predict the older child's reaction. He is likely to rush over and whirl by her, as if to say, "Look at me, too." To their surprise, though, he may not touch her. He may even resist pushing her down from her standing perch. But she topples anyway, just from watching him whiz by.

He has been watching her closely, and learning at the same time. He has learned how unsteady she feels as she tries to venture out, and how little he needs to do to thwart her. How easily he can sabotage her without getting caught. Twirling by her keeps her from daring to let go. Ingenious!

As a result, the baby may have to delay walking as much as a month or two after she's ready. Or she may have to figure out that she can brave a step when he's not nearby. Either way, she, too, is learning. How resourceful, and how much steadier she'll be when she does get going! She will be learning the skill of balancing, and to value that skill, from her hero worship of him. She wants to be on her feet, just like him.

The baby is beginning to ask a question that will haunt her for a long time: "When will I ever catch up to him?" The younger child will always long to catch up with the older one. She will try to stand, to toddle, to keep up with him. When she falls, her frustration may well bring on a tantrum. Not only has she failed, but she's failed to live up to him.

A parent can encourage the older child to hold the baby's hand when the infant tries to take a step. This may spur both of them to enjoy her mastery of walking. Stay nearby, though, but as inconspicuously as possible. He could easily speed up and pull her down. A baby of this age is not ready to stand up for herself. But the less you are involved, the less often their tussles will result in chaos.

Look for the changes in her ability to signal to him and to handle him. She will have learned ways of attracting him and of defending herself. Many younger children put up their hands as if to protect themselves, or they let out a squeal when the older child comes near. When you see these defensive reactions, you are likely to feel extra protective of the baby because she has to put up with such rough treatment at the hands of an older child. You are likely to feel a surge of anger.

The baby may not speak in words yet, but this is her way of saying to him, "Be careful, I'm little." Look at the baby's gestures as her way of encouraging her older sibling to play with her as well as to protect herself from his sudden impulses. Be nearby, just in case her protest sets off an overreaction from him. Any new step on her part may enrage him.

So when you can, hold back. You can watch and enjoy their learning about each other. As she walks, he takes her hand. When she falls, he may go to comfort her. Or he may not. He may feel so guilty about some of his wishes that he falls apart, too. One of our daughters would fall down beside her younger sister after making her fall. She was trying to undo her "mean-ness" and turn it into a game. As soon as she did, they both went into gales of laughter.

When there is a larger age gap, the older child may not feel as threatened by a baby sibling's new mobility. The older child may be far more competent at setting up and protecting his own play areas and at involving the baby in his play, or at keep-ing her out. But don't count on it. Parents are often amazed to discover how much rivalry even a much older child can feel, and how spitefully it can be expressed. This child, too, will need extra attention, and appreciation of his own recent new gains, when the baby begins to walk.

18 Months

As the baby becomes a toddler, she and her sibling will discover many new ways of playing together. Peekaboo and hiding. A 4-year-old and his 18-month-old sister imitate each other as they march around. This is a reward for their battles. They have a hilarious time throwing food off the table. The older one learns to skip. The toddler tries, but gets her feet tangled. They both laugh until they're breathless and red in the face. Their heightened awareness of each other's bodies is evidence of the powerful attachment they are developing.

A 4-year-old is fascinated now with differences, and needs to learn about them. He will want to examine her body when they are in the tub together. Of course, she will want to look at his penis and to touch it. This may cause an erection. If so, you'll be horrified. If you can stay out of it as much as possible, they'll soon get used to each other's differences. The exploration will lose its novelty, and the acts of touching will lose their excitement.

Few of us can stay out of it, however. Without stirring up more curiosity, a parent might calmly say, "That's her body. You have your penis outside. She has her wee-wee on the inside." At 3½ or 4 years, a child will be wondering about these differences and appreciate your contributions to his understanding.

This is the time to introduce the concept of privacy. If a child is excited and confused by the physical sensations aroused by the touching that he and his sister engage in, a parent can help settle this by setting some guidelines: "You can touch your own body when you're by yourself. It feels nice. And she can touch hers. But your body is private and so is hers. So you leave hers alone and make sure she leaves yours alone." If the older child senses that their touching makes the grownups around him frantic, he's bound to wonder why. He'll want to find out by persisting with his poking and probing. If, for any reason, the touching continues, this may be a time for parents to quietly set up separate, private bath times for each child—without a lot of fuss.

Should Siblings Share the Same Bedroom?

You may not have a choice, but if they share the same bedroom, expect your young children to climb in and out of each other's beds. The baby may still be in a crib, but the older child can often climb over the sides and get in with her. It is comforting and cozy to have company, but it's not safe for both children to be in the baby's crib. It's not sturdy enough to support all that weight. Forbidding it may make too much of it, but you can insist that they play together only in the older child's bed, which should be low enough to the ground to prevent injuries. Always be on the alert for safety. No pillows, no loose bedclothes, or toys in bed with them that could cause an accident. Unconscious aggressive feelings can surface at night, as well as caring ones. Allowing them to sleep in the same room before their competitive feelings are under control can be chancy.

At bedtime, children are bound to seek closeness with each other as they face separation from their parents. And at 4 years, the older child will be entering a time of fears, witches, and monsters. The toddler may be a comfort for him. Or she may call up in him new feelings that are behind these fears. A 4-year-old's fears arise from his new awareness of his own aggressive feelings, including ones about a younger sibling.

More Competence, More Competition

Along with the new rewards of a real playmate, the toddler also brings the older sibling a new threat. Not only can she now move into his space, she can also begin to compete on his turf. She can't live up to him, of course; but now she can try. And he knows it.

"She took my Lego and hid it." Every game they play together seems to end in a fight. How much should parents be involved? The toddler wants to be rescued, and the older child wants to be reassured that you recognize his superior prowess.

If you have been nearby enough to watch the buildup, you may know how each one has contributed to it. She seduces him with her almost unobservable biddings. He is all ready to respond. He takes over and bosses her around. She reacts with a half joyous, half protective squeal: an enticing but confusing message that he can't resist. That sets the tone. He starts tickling her, and won't stop even when he's pushed her over the edge. Her laughs become screams for a parent. If the parent tries to figure out who is to blame (hopeless) or takes on the children's job of learning to settle their own conflicts, their struggles will intensify.

Though they may not have planned it, the children will discover what a thrill it is to draw a parent into their squabbles. The triangle is more exciting than a twosome. As the toddler learns how to be a "victim" and the older child tries out the rewards of teasing the younger one, the presence of a parent adds drama to their play. It is very hard for a parent to stay out of it.

When my younger brother and I were little, we knew exactly how to get our mother off the phone, how to call her in from outside or from another room. I can remember the plotting look we would share with each other. Then, we'd go to work. My calling her didn't always bring her, but a few screeches from my brother worked every time.

Defusing Persistent Squabbles

- Be sure the younger one is safe. Remove dangerous toys, and separate the children if hitting gets out of control.
- Divert the older child with an interesting project or peers to play with.
- Help the older child with his anger by talking with him and helping him understand it, by reading stories about angry situations, or by playing out angry feelings with puppets or action figures. (See *Books for Children,* listed in the *Bibliography.*)
- After stopping a fight that has gotten out of control, hug each one and give them reassurance: "You can handle it with each other. I'm here to help when you need me. But it's your job to learn to get along with each other."

Older children (6 or 7) aren't as likely to have prolonged squabbles with a toddler sibling. Instead of wanting to compete, they may recognize their superiority and their ability to nurture. But they may tease as they brush by, or even set up a complex trap for the younger child. Then they'll chortle as the trap gets its victim. They can be merciless as they test their prowess and the younger child's resourcefulness.

Two children who are close in age (2 years apart or less) are more likely to spend long hours in fights with each other. Their persistence, their inventiveness, and their tolerance for the repetitious sparring reflect their need to test each other, and to learn how to handle themselves. In the early years, the fighting is also the result of the children's limited abilities to share, take turns, tolerate frustration, put off gratification, negotiate, and compromise. Parents can help them—with patience and repetition—to learn these new skills without trying to determine who started it, or which child is at fault.

2 to 3 Years

When a younger sibling is 2 or 3, she can be even more of a playmate for the older one, even if there is an age gap of 2 years or more. However, the 2- or 3-year-old may now be more reluctant to be the older child's "baby" or plaything. And an older sibling, at 5 or 6, might take advantage of the younger child's devout worship in different, perhaps more insidious ways.

A Secret Language
By the time the younger child turns 2, shared words and gestures have deepened the siblings' intimacy. They have developed their own language without words. Look at your two children as they interact. Watch their intensely practiced and subtle ways of communicating, and of keeping in touch. They are so aware of each other that they can signal their presence to each other in ways that no one else would ever notice. I once watched as a

5-year-old sat in his classroom, absorbed in his work. Though he never looked up, he instantly knew when his 3-year-old sister walked in. "There's Addie," he said matter-of-factly, still looking at his book. She'd made no perceptible noise, said nothing, but he knew. Such awareness seems almost extra-sensory.

Imitation

Watch the imitation between two siblings at this age. When one child begins to strut or to march proudly as if in a parade, the other will. Once, while working with a Native American tribe's Early Head Start Center, we were honored to be invited to a pow wow. Two siblings, 3 and 5 years, were dancing at opposite ends of the gymnasium. The older one jumped, twirled around, and marched along. From all the way across the room, the 3-year-old studied every move he made, imitating him clumsily but almost precisely—and almost on cue. I hadn't known they were siblings until I saw that performance, when it became perfectly apparent.

What does all this imitation mean to the older child? He is watched, envied, copied, followed around all day. Although it's flattering, it is also pretty hard to take. When his friends come over, the younger one wants to insert herself into their play and their relationships. When he tries to be alone, she is there. When he wants to get involved in more mature pastimes, she pulls on him. His guilt about deserting her, and his secret sadness at abandoning her, are lurking just below the surface. She can and will play on it.

Pushing Each Other's Limits

Meanwhile, the meltdowns caused by their rivalry are proceeding apace. Interfering with each other's play and bidding for parents' attention, they just can't stay out of each other's business. Tripping each other. Rolling around on the floor. Splashing each other in the tub. Flicking food at each other across the table. "I want as much ice cream as he got. One more spoonful." "No, you gave her more!" Through their constant scuffles, they seem to be saying, "I want to be part of your every moment."

The older child has an unfair advantage. When he decides he's had enough he can retreat to his room and slam the door. The 2-year-old, despondent, may throw herself on the floor in a flood of tears. Can you equalize their differences? Of course not. Once you've separated them, you can treat each one as an individual. You can help each one to settle down. Both will push parents to take sides. Don't do it. Instead, you can sympathize, and then ask each child to think about his or her role in the conflict.

To the older child, a parent might say, "I know it's tough to have your little sister interfering all the time, but you can tell her to stop, or take your toys into your room and shut the door. You don't have to hit." To the younger child, a parent might say, "I know you want to play with him *so* badly. But when he tells you he won't, you're going to have to learn to listen." Let her know you understand how hard that is for her, but that you can't change it. Over time, this will help her to stop idolizing her older sibling and to start sticking up for herself. Right now, though, she's bound to fall apart.

Prepare for Meltdowns at These Predictable Times:

- early morning, on the way to breakfast
- at the table
- shopping
- when homework piles up
- attention to one child (nursing, reading, special help)
- bedtime
- birthday party of one sibling
- Christmas and holidays with gifts and commotion
- long trips

Disciplining Children of Different Ages

How can parents respond to sibling conflicts when each child is at such a different developmental stage? It usually works out best to hold them both responsible for settling their struggles on their own. Yet the older child may be the only one who knows all the rules, or he may have an unfair advantage in their negotiations. One may be old enough to be expected to control himself, and the other still too young for such expectations. Each one may have a different motivation for misbehaving. Holding them responsible for working it out must include the fair handling of their differences.

One option is to send the children off to resolve their conflict on their own, and ask them to report back when they have done so. This strategy will help the older child control his urge to misuse his unfair advantages. It can also be an opportunity to help them both think about fairness. A parent might say, for example, "Look. I'm not going to get involved in figuring out who was right and who was wrong. You two need to figure it out. When you've come up with a solution that you're both satisfied with, then I'll be glad to listen." This sets up expectations for discipline for the whole family, not just for one child at a time. If it is clear that the older child has coerced the younger one, or if the children's efforts to sort things out end in a fight, a parent can suggest a few solutions and ask them to consider the fairness of each one. Both children are held responsible for making the solution work, even when only one is guilty of having created the problem.

Disciplining Children with Different Temperaments

To add to the challenge of disciplining children of different ages at the same time, parents will also need to take into account the different temperaments of each child. In some situations, blanket rules apply. For example, "No chores, no allowance," or "Say you're sorry." Parents may feel that it isn't "fair" to treat a very sensitive child with one kind of discipline and the other with more active restrictions. Yet when parents understand the role of temperament in a child's misbehavior and how he can learn from it, they'll see that discipline needs to be fitted to each child accordingly. Discipline that teaches will often need to be adapted to the child's temperament as well as to the crime.

With a quiet, sensitive child, it may suffice after a tantrum to sit her down quietly to hold her and rock her until she calms. She is learning ways to calm herself. With the more active sibling who won't sit in your lap, you may need to send him to his room; but offer your lap and rocking chair when *he* feels ready. He, too, is learning ways to settle himself that will work for him.

But how do you explain to each child the differences in the discipline that each receives? You know you are bound to hear such remarks as "But that's not fair. How come I always get punished and she doesn't?" A parent can explain: "Fairness does not mean the same thing for everyone, but the right thing for each of you. Fairness means doing what I have to do to help each of you learn your lesson. If you learn quickly, I don't need to use time outs or punishments." It is easier to help the children accept this when parents themselves understand that though fairness means the same rules, it may not mean the same discipline for every child. Instead, discipline will need to fit each child's readiness to learn.

Touchpoints of Development—Second Time Around

Many steps that are difficult for the first child to learn are a cinch for the second. Toilet training a second child is often easy. The second child is always hungrily watching and learning from the first. She is usually so motivated to keep up with the first one that she will pick up each step by imitat ion. If children are close in age and the first one is lagging, she's likely to surge ahead as if to say, "See, I can do it even if you can't." Pressure on the older child from the younger one is almost bound to contribute to the older child's frustration and perhaps to further delays.

Meanwhile, the younger child has finally found a way to excel: "I can poop in the toilet and you can't." What a triumph! And what a devastatingly humbling experience for the older one. The motivation behind the younger one's success is obvious. You may be tempted to use this new pressure on the older child to get him going with toilet training. Don't. Instead, reassure him that you can accept his lack of readiness in this area, and his feelings about it: "Isn't it a pain in the neck to have your little sister train herself when you aren't ready yet? You know, she's always having to put up with you being able to do everything else before she is. No wonder she wanted to make a big deal about this. Don't worry. When you're ready, you'll poop in the toilet, too."

And to her: "I know you're proud of pooping in the toilet all by yourself, and I'm proud of you, too. But how do you think it makes your brother feel? You can be proud of yourself and still pay attention to how he feels." In this way, a parent can turn siblings' competition into an opportunity to understand each others' feelings, and to care about them. This is surely not a time to compare siblings or to pit one against the other.

Understanding Brother-Sister Differences

Watch a girl try to stand up at the toilet to be like her older brother. Let a younger sister, who has been watching an older brother, sit on the toilet facing in, so she can see herself urinate (see our book *Toilet Training: The Brazelton Way,* Da Capo, 2004). This is a beginning of her awareness of gender differences. She may announce that she expects her penis to grow in any day now, or she may storm around and get worked up about unrelated things as a result. (When she was born, her brother—having caught a glimpse of an early diapering session—may have concluded that his might fall off at any moment!) In these years, a child is just beginning to sort out his or her gender identity. If the older sibling is a girl, a little boy may want to sit on the toilet "to pee like her." He may even be surprised that he overshoots, but she doesn't. (When he sees his father stand at the toilet, his whole approach will quickly change.)

The strong attachment to one parent and then to the other that occurs at this age, and in the years to come, is an attempt to learn about and to absorb parts of each parents' identity. This same fervor to absorb the gender and characteristics of the parents will invade their sibling relationship, especially when both children fall into the 3-to-6 age range. The younger sister will try to dress like her older brother. She may try to copy his swagger, to use dirty words the way he does, to ignore his parents' requests. All will be learned in an effort to be just like him. The frustration when it isn't possible will come out as jealousy, or as denial that she can't really be like him. I would expect a younger sibling to waver between anger and sadness when she must face the reality: "I'll never be like him. I'll never be a boy. I'll never be the person I want to be."

A little boy is likely to imitate his older sister, and to want to play with dolls. He'll try out dressing like her, or will want to play with her friends. A little boy's admiring identification still seems to bother parents more than when a girl imitates so-called typical male behavior. Parents may overreact and worry that he won't ever learn to think of himself as a boy. He may need more time with other boys his age, as well as with his father, but his imitation of his sister is his way of admiring her and learning from her.

The Older Sibling's Vulnerability

By 4 or 5 years of age, the older sibling has a new awareness of his angry feelings toward his little sibling. (See *Touchpoints Three to Six,* listed in the *Bibliography.*) When he was younger, he could blithely reach out to swat or sabotage her. But now he feels torn. Of course he still wants to tease her, but now he knows more clearly than before that it is wrong to hurt her and feels guilty when he does. Meanwhile, the younger child will provoke him into lashing out again. Even this kind of attention makes her want more. She wants his approval, his willingness to treat her like a peer. She wants to *be* him. But she can't. Her tantrums are a likely result.

At the same time, the younger child is able to set off a melt-down in her older brother more easily now, too. She becomes aware of his sensitive spots, and she is all too likely to want to play on them. As he becomes more and more aware of his aggressive feelings, he becomes more upset about how close to losing control he can be. He wants to get rid of her all over again. "Mom, keep her away from me!" He may try to avoid his little sister if she succeeds in setting him off too often.

I remember running away—down the street to my grandmother's house—to escape from my younger brother. My grandmother was always glad to see me and she made me feel special. I thought I was punishing my parents as I labored under the illusion that they didn't know where I was.

But how could a 5-year-old today get away safely? He'll long more than ever for a space all his own that the younger child can't invade. If they've been sharing a room, it may be time to try to separate them, if possible. If not, create a space for him, perhaps a table and shelves that only he can use on a porch, or in a corner of another room. Help him make "KEEP OUT" signs to hang in this space, showing him how to write them.

A child of this age also needs peers of his own. As he struggles with angry feelings towards a younger sibling, having a friend who has a younger sibling and must deal with the same issues will be especially important to him. A playmate for the younger one will help keep her from tagging along with them.

Listen to the older ones as they share their gripes: "That baby gets in my way every time I try to do anything. If I want to throw a ball or play catch, she has to be there. Dad and Mom won't do anything. I get so sick of her." "Me, too. Mine makes me so mad I pinch her. Then I run out the door. They don't even know what happened to her. Sometimes I wish I could lose her on the street. Or run away." "Me, too."

Parents wonder what has happened to their nurturing older child. "He was so great with her before. Now, all of a sudden, he hates her. He teases her and shoves her. What can I do about it? The more I scold him, the more he misbehaves, and the sneakier he becomes. Sometimes he seems depressed. He says things like, 'I wish I could live somewhere else' or 'I wish I were dead.' That really scares me." What has happened to him? At this age, a child can be overwhelmed by both his anger toward his younger sibling and his guilty feelings about it.

At times, the older child may try to control his feelings, or make up for them, by "loving her to death." He'll smother her with unwanted attention. He'll interfere in everything she tries to do. He'll try to absorb her attention away from everyone else.

Parents are surprised and confused when the older child's sadness, fearfulness, and withdrawal occur right alongside his smothering love *and* his open aggression toward the younger child. It helps to understand that this is his time both for a new dawning awareness of aggressive feelings and a new need to control them. This behavior surfaces in the fourth and fifth year, and is frightening to the child, especially if there is a target for angry feelings such as a younger sibling.

Ghosts from the Nursery

Parents are likely to remember their own feelings from the past. If one was the first child, he or she will remember an old wish to be the only child all over again. If a parent was the younger child growing up, the need to protect the "baby" is likely to surface.

This makes it very hard to be objective about the turmoil and the fighting that occurs. Memories of difficult times with siblings may lead parents to try to "settle" disputes, to take sides in the battle, and to try to make things fair. Taking one side or the other is unlikely to succeed. One child or the other will cry out, "You love her better than me." Parents' awareness of their "ghosts" can make it easier to stop for a moment before reacting, and to reach for a wider range of responses.

3 to 4 Years

As an older child enters first grade, the importance of friends will pull him away from a younger sibling. The older sibling may be painfully clear: "Mom, no one wants to come over to my house. They know *she'll* have to tag along. I can't stand it any longer. She's like a leech. I can't ever get away from her. She makes me crazy and all the kids know it."

Parents will understand why he needs space from his adoring sister. But how can they help him while protecting her? She does adore him. She wants to be part of the group as much as he does. She wants to be *him.* She walks like him. She tries to dress like him. (He even locks himself in the bathroom in the morning to get dressed so that she can't see what he's going to wear.) She talks like him, using the same slang and the same inflections. No wonder his complaints about her tagging along

Helping Siblings to Become Individuals—and to Stay Close

- Woo a close friend or two for the younger sibling.
- Assure the younger child that the older one doesn't mean to reject her, but needs time with friends on his own now.
- Let older children gravitate to friends their own age.
- Don't pressure the older child to nurture a younger one (he is more likely to do so on his own).
- Avoid criticizing.
- Commend an older child who does care for a younger one.
- Listen to both children. You can value each child's perspective without taking sides. With your listening, you help them listen to each other. By taking each child seriously, you help them take each other seriously.
- Then let them know your stance: "The two of you will have to work this out yourselves."
- Leave as much problem solving as possible to the children.
- When they need help, let the older child help the younger one (and you) by offering suggestions.
- Offer privacy and special times for each child.
- Make sure there are regular mealtimes and other family rituals that bring siblings together.
- Plan regular family meetings. Lay down rules, chores, expectations, and consequences; these help children feel part of the working family.

continues on next page

Helping Siblings to Become Individuals—and to Stay Close
continued from previous page

- Set limits and stick with them: "That's the way we do it in our family." Over time, you can help them understand why. But before they can, they must understand that "that's the way it is."
- Avoid comparisons, avoid babying the baby, or over-praising the older one.
- Support their efforts to include each other, but don't pressure them. "You have your friends. He has his. That's important right now."
- Don't expect their conflicts to go away. Ever.
- Do expect them to stand up for each other, to make sacrifices for each other, and to care deeply about each other.

don't seem to touch her. She makes him want to scream. He asks permission to go to a friend's house just to avoid her. Otherwise, he knows she'll be there, waiting, wrecking his chances of being part of the group.

Other children who have younger siblings seem to understand. They talk together about ways they could get rid of their younger siblings. But they won't tell each other how guilty they feel about wanting to. Parents will know they do, though, when they see the other side. On holidays or weekends, when there's no chance of his friends showing up, the older sibling will fall back on his old nurturing stance—some of the time. He'll show her how to play video games. He'll even play card games with her. He may bring magic tricks home that he's learned from his friends to teach her so she can show everyone in her class "when she's big enough." He may even laugh, instead of blowing up, when she tries to cheat. Now, secretly, he is proud of her.

Even when a younger sibling is 4 or 5 years old, there are still plenty of blowups. There is always competition. Each child vies to have his or her needs met in the family. Each child continues to try for the other's approval, too. There is always caring, though it isn't always easy to see. By 7 or 8 years the older child's interests have begun to shift beyond the family, but his ties to siblings and parents can be a strong base to launch from. Stronger than he's ever likely to let on to when the world beckons.

CHAPTER 3

Common Challenges in Sibling Relationships

Adopted Siblings

Parents who decide to adopt must have powerful motivations. These need to be understood because such motivations are bound to influence the family's adjustment to the adoption.

Many adoptive parents will need to deal with the doubts and sorrows that have accompanied them through fertility work-ups, in vitro fertilization and other procedures, and the adoption process. Later, as long as the adoptive child is on a rewarding developmental track, and parents' efforts to bond with the child are successful, these feelings need not resurface. But, when the parents' efforts go astray or are not rewarded, or when the child goes through a "touchpoint" (a temporary slide backward before a new developmental step) they will again be vulnerable to doubt and worry. Siblings will pick up on these worries.*

What Siblings Need to Know

Adoptive parents who expect the inevitable, normal challenges and regressions of childhood will be less troubled by them (though they'll still want to know whether there are other causes). Otherwise, their anxiety and even a sense of failure will be likely to affect the whole family. Siblings will sense their parents' concerns about the adopted child, and this in turn will affect the way they see the sibling.

Different Feelings for Different Children

Adoptive parents who have biological children may discover that they feel differently about their biological children and the adopted one. They may have to face these emotional reactions when dealing with sibling rivalry. How painful to discover underlying feelings about the adopted child, for example, "He's an outsider. My child comes first." When parents notice how their reactions to an adopted child differ, they might think they should suppress these feelings. Although children need to be treated fairly, different reactions are bound to arise and need to be faced squarely.

---

*In Chapter Three, we will use "she" for the older child and "he" for the younger one.

Of course, you feel differently. Parents are affected differently by each child, biological or adopted. Can you treat them alike? Probably not. Hiding your feelings from yourself won't hide them from your children. They will sense your attempt to compensate—either by favoring the adopted child, or by ignoring the siblings' feelings.

When children in a family have been adopted from different parents, they may ask about their birth parents from time to time. But they aren't likely to pay that much attention to such differences in the first years. By 4 or 5 years, however, children begin to notice them and may tease each other about their differences and about being adopted. But because each child is vulnerable in one way or another, this teasing isn't likely to last. Instead, after learning about each other's reactions to such teasing, they have the chance to become protective of each other, and accepting of each other's differences.

The difficult job for parents will be to match their reactions to each child's needs. Not easy. To do this, they'll need to take into account the child's temperament, age, behavior, and, for a child adopted after infancy, earlier experiences as well.

Preparing Siblings for an Adoption

Before a new sibling is adopted, children in the family need help in understanding this decision. First, it must be clear that it is the parents' decision, not theirs. They mustn't be made to feel responsible, even if they've begged for a baby sister or brother. Otherwise, when they later discover their other feelings—the resentful, jealous ones—they'll be confused and may even won-der whether they can decide to "disadopt."

Instead, before the adoption, the children need a chance to become aware of and share their feelings—excitement, indiffer-ence, uncertainty, longing, and fears. The adoption of a new sibling can certainly feel like an invasion. If concerns such as these can be aired in advance, children are less likely to act on them in ways they'll later regret.

Understanding Siblings' Fears

Siblings may feel, as their parents do, that they must nurture and help "this child who hasn't his own mommy and daddy" or who is "different" or has special needs. They are bound to fear that they will lose their own mommy and daddy as he has, or if he has a disability, that something might damage them, too. They might even feel that this is just a rehearsal for their par-ents to put *them* up for adoption. When a child hears about a mother's "giving up" her baby, why wouldn't she worry that she will be "traded in" for the adopted child? Now she'll really have to stifle her jealous feelings and be "extra good."

For siblings, adjusting to an adopted child is different from adjusting to a baby who is born into the family. A newborn is fragile and needs special care. But an adopted child brings a story, one of loss and abandonment that must be made up for. To bring such a child into the family amounts to asking the other children to take an almost parental stance toward that child. "Help us take care of this special child," the act of adoption seems to be saying. They will need help accepting that they won't always live up to this.

Different Kinds of Adoptions

There are so many different kinds of adoption—for example, open adoptions, adoption of two or more children from the same background, cross-cultural adoption, the adoption of a child with identified or suspected special needs. All this must be shared in advance with siblings, and in terms they can understand.

They will need to understand the child's strengths and weaknesses, how they can help, and the limits of their help. They will need to know that they can count on their parents to care for this child in ways that they cannot, to protect them from feeling overly responsible. The goal will be to help them recognize the challenges of an adoption and value the rewards, while leaving room for them to voice their misgivings and to live their own lives. A fine line!

Adopted Siblings' Vulnerability

When an adopted child is stressed by family issues, including challenging relationships with siblings, or by predictable touchpoints of development, he will be likely to regress to earlier memories and behavior. A child may melt down, or become violent and out of control, as he relives the memory of events from his past. He is bound to try out his worst behavior to test his deepest fear: that he's too "bad" for any family to accept him. He'll even push his new parents to face their feelings with disruptive behavior that asks: "Can you really want me as much as your 'own' children?" This vulnerability will make sibling understanding more difficult, and more important.

Whenever there is a family crisis, or even a touchpoint, familiar questions are bound to come up for parents all over again: "Should we have done it? They fight all the time. Was it fair to our biological children to have done it?" Parents will need to settle such questions for themselves if they are to help siblings understand the adopted child's regressions.

Parents can then help siblings understand the adopted child's behavior. They might say, for example, "He gets frightened and upset when he remembers what happened to him before he came to us. Now that he feels safe with us, he can let out these feelings and these fears. That's why he screams out at night. Or acts mean to you."

Before assuming anything, listen to the siblings' reactions to the adopted child's behavior, and their questions. These will guide you as you try to help them understand and accept the new child. Your acceptance of their fears and protests will serve as a model of tolerance for them.

A Sibling's Questions

Bringing an adoptive child into a family will be likely to raise the biological children's own questions: "Am I really their child, or was I adopted? I'd better be good, or they may give me up. Why wasn't I enough to please them?"

At crisis times, such as meltdowns, sibling conflicts, or the predictable regressions of the adoptive child, siblings may feel that they should smooth them over, or take responsibility. Either would be costly in the long run. There is also the risk that they might explode and say hateful things that they'll later regret, and that the adopted child will hold onto as confirmation of her worst fears. Yet there must be times when the other children are able to blow off steam.

The more you can encourage the siblings of an adopted child to speak freely with you, the easier it will be for them. You can help them accept their jealous and competitive feelings as natural and inevitable. "Of course he drives you crazy. He's little and gets in your way. You know how to get him where it really hurts because you're his sister. But you feel terrible when you do—because he's your brother!" There is also bound to be the usual testing: "I hate that kid. Why did you get him? Can't you take him back?" Other common though often unspoken questions parents will want to be aware of: "Do I have to like him? You always make me take care of him. How about me?"

Sooner or later, the biological child will tease: "You're adopted and I'm not." Don't overreact. Instead, be prepared for the full range of feelings that adoption calls up. Regular one-to-one discussions for each child with parents will help all the siblings, adopted and biological, live with these feelings and with each other. You can't force them to care about each other. But if you honor all their feelings, even the negative ones, they'll be more likely to find room in their hearts for the positive ones.

Cross-Racial and Cross-Cultural Adoptions

At 4 and 5 years, children become curious about differences. At this age, they don't understand what they might mean to others. As they wonder, they're likely to blurt out: "You look different. You're not even from America."

A parent's reaction will be to rush in to help. Don't. But let each child know you won't tolerate hurtful teasing. Then, encourage each child to ask questions about the differences they notice. If the adopted child is of a different background, be sure he meets older children and adults from his own race or culture whom he can admire. He may well need them to identify with and to balance his feelings of being "different" from his siblings.

Children may not be as interested in their adopted sibling's culture as their parents are: "You keep talking about his culture and his problems. How about mine?" Commitment to each other in the long run is the goal. But this may be best achieved by leaving the children room to balance caring about each other with their own independent lives. As in biological families, rivalry and learning about each other go hand-in-hand. Both sides are necessary to the development of a passionate relationship.

The adopted child will need your help with his feelings about his siblings because he's bound to have negative feelings about them: "They're so lucky. They'll never really accept me or love me as much as they love each other. They couldn't really want me, just like my 'real' family didn't. My sister would be happier if I weren't around. She just feels sorry for me." When the adopted child has more than one sibling, he may feel left out. "I wish they'd play with me the way they do with each other. Why won't they lie next to me on the floor the way they do with each other? I wish I were one of them. Will I ever be?" He's bound to feel all this, and more. How much harder it is for an adopted child to ever say such feelings out loud!

For parents of an adopted child, there is an added responsibility in sorting out sibling relationships. All your children will learn most about caring for each other from modeling on you. When you can demonstrate fairness, respect, and caring deeply about each one as an individual, it sets the tone for the children—biological and adoptive. It isn't easy. Don't let the inevitable glitches discourage you.

Birth Order

Birth order is often used—both by children and by parents—to explain siblings' different personalities. Siblings will even use birth order to blame and negotiate. "She's the baby, and everyone treats her that way. Ugh! I can't stand her." Or to the oldest, younger siblings might demand: "Couldn't you be nicer to us and share your clothes? You have so many." Of course, being the first, last, or in the middle will influence each child's behavior.

But it is harder to use birth order to predict who a child will become than some may think. So many other factors determine personality, too—how many years there are between siblings, their gender, not to mention each child's temperament, and the whole range of life experiences. No wonder different birth order researchers seem to come up with different results.

Oldest Child

Everyone expects the oldest to grow up quickly. The other children treat her with respect but also expect her to be more generous, more helpful than she may want to be. When she grows tired of her "older child role," she may turn on them. "Leave me alone. Stop bugging me." This may feel like a desertion if the younger sibling is used to being nurtured and cared for by her.

An oldest child may be expected to be an athlete or a "brain." "Help me with my homework. You've already learned how to do it. And anyway, you're the smart one in the family." She may feel flattered by this kind of adoration, and she'll do her best—for a while.

But she may also feel the pressure of this role, and rebel. She may turn on a younger sibling and treat him mercilessly. She may even take out on him the anger she feels about her parents' pressure for her to be the "oldest and most responsible." For example, when she's asked to baby-sit, she may find a way to dodge the role, or she may make a sibling's life so miserable that she isn't asked again.

Helping the Oldest Child
Handle Responsibility

- Try not to expect the oldest to be "too" responsible. Watch for signs of needing relief from the role. Even if there is a large gap, don't expect the older one to do all the babysitting.
- Praise the older child for the responsibility she demonstrates at times when you have not requested it. But be aware that too much praise represents pressure.
- Value the older child for her uniqueness in the family, independent from any expectation for her to be the "oldest and the most responsible." "I love it when you come in to sit on my bed and tell me about your day. It's just like you were my little girl again when we used to cuddle and talk over everything you'd done."
- Let the oldest be a baby, too, when she needs to. Pushing an older child too soon to give up sucking her thumb, or carrying her blanket everywhere, or other "babyish" behaviors is bound to backfire. Expect her to fall back on these under pressure, and let her know that such temporary backsliding is okay.
- Try to free the older child up from her siblings enough to have friends of her own, outside the family.

No matter how the oldest child behaves, she is likely to be a role model for younger siblings. Watch a toddler become hooked on an older child's ball throwing. He'll shape his hands in imitation, even if he must still throw with both hands. His eyes and his adoration show how much he values the older child as a teacher.

A younger sibling follows the oldest one around like a puppy dog. Often, this behavior is carried to extremes, and it is not appreciated. "Mom, don't let that little squirt come out of the house when my friends come over. He always ruins our games. But he talks my friends into letting him play anyway. I'm so embarrassed I just want to go somewhere else to play." And, yet, at other times, the older child teaches her siblings the games she plays with her friends. A mixed blessing and a mixed role for the eldest. A lot of responsibility, whether she likes it or not.

An oldest girl is expected to be a second mother, a boy a second father and teacher. When the oldest tries to fight off this role, everyone is shocked. The oldest feels surprised and guilty. The younger ones feel abandoned. Predictably, the older child's teaching and helping will be rebuffed, at other times, by the younger child. "I don't need you. I can do it myself."

Middle Child

A middle child starts out as the youngest sibling, and was the oldest child's "baby." He has worked hard to find his niche in the family, both wooing and competing with the older child. Suddenly, another baby comes along. Everyone is ecstatic. Everyone except him. All of them concentrate on this new baby—including the older child. The middle child is deserted by everyone, including his rival, whom he can no longer even provoke into a squabble. If a younger child becomes a middle child, the hardest part may be the "desertion" of the older child, who will turn to the new baby. The older child will no longer be as available to play or fight.

The second child is now a "middle child." With everyone, including his older sibling, concentrating on the new baby's latest antics, a middle child feels as if the rug were pulled out from under him. To him, being in the middle feels like being forgotten. He may try to provoke, to show off, to cry out for someone—anyone. Unless a parent hears this cry, he continues to be without a sounding board, without a reliable advocate. Some middle children learn to turn their wish to be cared for into caring for others—later.

A middle child may try to make up for his loneliness with friends. But he may seem irritable, and depressed. He may want to run away. He picks at his food, wakes up at night. He gets fed up with the dog, but he loves the dog. Parents will ask, "Why are you so upset? Isn't she a cute baby? Look at her watch you, adoring you." Of course, she looks at everybody that way because they all adore her. The eyes and the winning smile everyone saves for the baby makes the middle child "want to puke." How could he ever like her?

In time, the middle child may start to mother the baby. But when the baby screeches, he wants to swat her over the head. But he doesn't, and soon he may find that he can woo the baby from his older sister. Not often, but just enough to make it worth the effort. When he fails, he'll battle with the little one.

Sibling rivalry is always near the surface. "Will they ever just get along?" parents wonder in desperation.

A middle child may continue to wish for a unique role such as "first" or "last." He may try even harder to live up to the oldest, or he may try to be entirely different, seeking his own niche. He may even play it for all he can. "You always give in to her. And you're always so proud of him. You treat me like a middle child." He is likely to provoke a response from his parents. They are aware of the label and of their own role in having labeled him.

But don't let the middle child make you feel guilty. The myth of the "middle child," and parents' worries about it, may be more powerful than its reality. My middle daughter can always get at me when she says, "You treat me like a middle child!" Do I? I don't think so, until she accuses me of it. The "book end" children do have special places (the eldest and the baby), but maybe the middle is a special place as well. A middle child isn't as likely to be as overwhelmed as the first child, nor as overprotected as the baby. It may be a freer spot to be in. One can always just disappear in a crisis. Some middle children even figure out how to use this position in the family to ensure that no one expects as much of them.

Some middle children find they have unique creative gifts that allow them to distinguish themselves from the first born in their families. Others will learn to be the peacemakers; they will mediate conflicts and feel responsible for everyone's well-being. They feel the pressure, but also the rewards of being in the middle. Our second child found her way by nurturing her baby brother, and she became invaluable.

When a middle sibling can define a necessary role for himself in the family, he feels needed and competent.

Helping the Middle Child Feel Valued

- Remind a middle child of his talents. Praise him for his resilience, in adjusting to the baby, and finding his own role.
- Let the middle child groan and complain—even blow up about how hard he works to be a contributing member of the family. As he feels heard, he will learn a lot about himself.
- Face whatever bias you may have about a middle child. Maybe it reminds you of your own past, or that of a family member. But remember, you've given him a family to care about, to compete with, and to fall back on.
- Don't feel sorry for him. Pity will only push a child to focus on the negative aspects of his situation. Every position in the family has its rewards and burdens. The give and take demanded of each child is the cement that makes the family strong.

The Last Child—the "Baby"

Everyone loves the baby—as long as he *is* the baby. He gets used to being adored. He knows when to dodge the sibling just above. The rest of the family makes allowances for the youngest child.

Then, all of a sudden, he begins to grow up. No longer do his babyish wiles help. When he battles over something he wants,

How to Help the Youngest Child Grow Up

- Value his struggle to keep up with older siblings.
- Comfort him when he needs it. But remember that the role of a baby cannot last. He needs to value the new abilities he can develop, even when he can't live up to his siblings.
- Remind yourself how much you love having a baby and how you may be prolonging his baby role.
- Be ready for his accusation: "You always treat me like a baby." You probably do. Apologize, and let him know that you'll try to stop, though you may not always succeed.

suddenly everyone labels him as "spoiled." His older siblings desert him. (They've waited patiently.) His behavior becomes the center of everyone's concern and discussion. He feels the loss of special privileges.

Now, he must face the music. He must compete successfully with his older siblings. Being cute doesn't cut it any more. The pressure to leave the "baby" role behind often weighs more heavily on boys than on girls; in girls, appeals of being "fragile" and "helpless" are still more likely to be tolerated.

In search of a niche, the youngest child may become a rebel, an unexpected performer. He may not fit in with the rest of the family's patterns. He can be unique and surprising. But if less has always been expected of him, he may learn to expect less of himself.

If the youngest regresses to baby-like behavior at home, it is still likely to draw his parents in. But he will pay the price of being the butt of his siblings' disapproval. He may then resort to bravado or rebellion. But when his siblings accept him, he blossoms. He will have learned a great deal about adapting to his more grown-up role, and about giving up his babyish one for new rewards.

Chronically Ill Siblings

Chronic illness in a child stretches the resources of a family. All kinds of adults may be in and out of the home to offer professional help or emotional support—to the sick child and to the parents. Everyone's attention is directed toward the chronically ill child. No one has energy left over for anything else, and siblings know it.

In a moment of weakness they might admit that they'd like to be the center of attention again. Just for a moment. But any bid for attention—negative or positive—calls up such exhausted leftover feelings in the parents that the effort is almost not worth it. The well child learns to keep her jealousy to herself. "How can you say something like that, when your brother is so ill? Suppose you were in pain like he is, would you want him to be jealous—or complain about you?"

A healthy child's feelings about a sick sibling lead to guilt: "Why is he sick? Is it my fault? I fought with him so much."

What to do with those intense feelings? A child can't live with them just boiling inside, but she may be able to learn to turn these guilty feelings into nurturing ones. She'll try to help out the people who care for her sibling. But she will worry about making mistakes. If she drops the juice on the bed, people might blame it on her angry feelings.

And if her sibling doesn't get better, she'll worry that she didn't wish hard enough for it. Rarely does anyone help a child escape from her feelings about a sick sibling. They stay with her all the time. Parents can watch for these feelings in a sibling. They can be aware of the child's wish to be "good" and helpful. Acknowledge how hard it is for her. "It must seem like no one pays any attention to you. Maybe you wonder if anyone knows how hard you are working to help out. I do, but I probably don't tell you I do often enough."

What else can help the healthy sibling? She can take a break and visit a friend. But even there, she faces such questions as "How's your brother? And how are your parents putting up with all they have to do?" Innocent questions like these can make the healthy child feel guilty. No one asks, "How are *you* putting up with it?"

Even a healthy child's best friend may be a little wary, as if the healthy child is a carrier for the sick sibling's illness, as if "it might rub off." When illness strikes, everyone is afraid that it could happen to him or her, and wonders why it hasn't. As a result, fears and superstitions crop up for children and adults alike. The fear of contagion is always there: "My brother got sick and now he can't walk. That might happen to me, too. I'm his sister." A sibling will worry, "I deserve to be sick more than my brother does. He's so good. And I'm not."

A child might even think, "If I got sick, maybe he'd get better." This kind of magical "bargaining" is a child's way of dealing with her own sad feelings. She's bound to feel like a failure for not being able to make her brother better, and to feel guilty because she "hates" him for "getting all the attention."

Some siblings develop a symptom like the sick child's. A healthy sibling might start limping or coughing or behave as if she had a pain in her belly. She might even feel that she does. But no one has any sympathy for that. They just look at the healthy child and wonder, "How could you?" And the healthy child may wonder too, "How could I? But I want to help him. I want to feel it like he does. I want to be him—to take it away from him." Or she may not be aware of the feelings beneath her symptoms. But, either way, no one understands. When the healthy sibling does try to help, the sick one looks up at her with such big sad eyes. It makes her feel even worse. It's easier to skip by the sick child's room as fast as she can.

A two-year-old we know was in a hospital, dying of a brain tumor. The nurses adored him and put him out in a playpen in the center of the floor so that everyone could speak to him lovingly when they passed by. He seemed too weak to really enjoy it. The nurses did it anyway—every day. It was the only way they could face the fact that they hadn't any other way to help him. One day, the toddler was lying in the corner of the open

Helping Children Handle Their Feelings About a Chronically Ill Sibling

1. Offer siblings enough information about the sick child's illness for them to understand that it is not their fault, that they did not cause it, and, if this is true, that they won't get the sick child's illness too.
2. Give siblings regular chores to help—not only the sick child but the whole household.
3. Watch a sibling's cues to see when she needs a special time away with one of the parents—just for fun, not for recapping the illness or focusing on the sick child.
4. Set up family meetings. Make time for family meals. Sing or just talk together to establish an atmosphere of family togetherness in spite of the stress you must all live with.
5. Parents should seek help for themselves if they become overwhelmed or depressed so that healthy siblings will not feel that they must take care not only of the sick child, but of fragile parents, too.
6. Some siblings may need therapy of their own to help them deal with the feelings a sick child stirs up in them. Sometimes hospitals offer groups for the siblings of sick children. There they will meet other children who want to help their siblings but who also feel jealous of all the attention that sickness brings. They can discover, without pressure to talk if they don't want to, that they are not alone with their confusing feelings of anger, sadness, fear, and guilt.

playpen, propped between two pillows. His parents got off the elevator and leaned over him to stroke him. He roused himself briefly to acknowledge them. Then he quieted.

Then, his two older brothers aged 4 and 6 got off the elevator. The toddler saw them. His eyes lit up. He crawled up to the side of the playpen nearest them. He pulled himself up to stand. He leaned out toward them, his face and eyes shining. As they patted him, he moaned, "Ooh! Ooh! Ooh!" We all watched with tears streaming down our faces. How much these older boys meant to this child! But it's difficult for well siblings to accept that kind of responsibility.

Children who learn to adjust in a family that copes together with a difficult situation gain many strengths. They are less likely to be vulnerable to peer pressure and to turn away from their family's values in adolescence. As they face one child's illness, the whole family can become stronger.

Comparisons

Parents are bound to compare their children with each other. It is inevitable. Why shouldn't they delight in their differences? "Isn't it amazing that we gave birth to such completely different children?" Helping the children deal with their differences, though, is another story. Comparisons, inevitable as they may be, won't help.

Watch a younger sibling gloat when the older one is in trouble; he'll be on his best behavior to milk his temporary advantage for as much as it's worth. It can be tempting for parents to use the "good behavior" of one child as an example for the other: "Why can't you listen and do as you're told like your brother?" Don't. It's bound to backfire.

Comparing siblings openly, or in any way that sets one up as "better" than another, puts all the children in a bind. "She's our star athlete!" Or, "He's the most thoughtful in the family." The "preferred" child knows he'll be the target of anger and envy, and the "lesser" ones are bound to feel discouraged. Comments from parents, such as "Why can't you learn to behave the way your brother does?" are likely to hurt in ways that are not intended, and to be remembered.

A kind of hopelessness can be generated in a child's mind: "He always does everything right. They really don't care when I try. I hate him." Some children may respond by giving up, some may be spurred on to try harder. But a child who feels less admired by a parent is unlikely to turn to that parent for help when he needs it. And even if such talk does motivate a child to compete with the favored sibling, are the lasting negative effects it may have on their relationship worth it?

Comparing children in this way can be destructive. Using superlatives, words such as "best, worst, last, most" can strike deep. Even when a parent wishes to commend one child, words such as "the greatest" and "the best" can unintentionally pit one child against the others. Try not to use such terms about one sibling to the other. It's hard to avoid, especially when one child acts out in a disappointing way. "Why can't you be more like your sister? She's always so neat?" Yet that kind of statement is almost sure to hurt more than it helps.

Talking About Shortcomings

When a parent must address a child's shortcomings, try focusing on that child alone—without comparisons to others. For an always-late child, for example, it might be tempting to say, "Your brother doesn't seem to have any trouble getting to school on time." Instead, a parent can wait for a calm moment to say, "I know it bothers you to be so rushed, and how much you want to be on time. If you need more time, you could get your stuff ready for school before you go to bed. Is there a way I could help you be on time?"

Your children will like themselves and each other more if they don't hear you compare them with each other. Of course, they already do it themselves. They are always aware of the differences between them, of each others' accomplishments and failures. But a parent's words weigh so much more heavily than their own. A child is much more likely to try to compensate for her own areas of weakness if you don't talk about them in front of the other children, if you don't discuss them in comparison to the other children's abilities in the same areas.

Instead, say, "I know that spelling is hard for you. But you are getting better at it, and I admire you for keeping on trying." Patience and perseverance are important qualities to value. It is easier for parents to hold back on comparisons when they've found something special to value about each child.

Talking with One Sibling About Another

Sometimes, one child will push a parent to talk about a sibling, often asking a parent to agree with the child's complaint: "She's so spoiled. She always gets her way. Don't you think she needs to learn she's not the only one in the world?" Certainly, a parent can listen and respond to the child's feelings: "She really bugs you, doesn't she?" But don't side with one child against another.

Instead, to help develop your child's capacity for empathy, encourage her to think about the other child's perspective. You might ask her, "What do you think is going on with her?" You needn't say what you think. If you do, keep it general, respectful, and hopeful. You are modeling a way for her to work out a relationship. If the other child does need your discipline, you can do that in private.

Talking About Differences

Avoiding comparisons doesn't mean, though, that families can't talk together about their differences. If one child has a unique talent, or a special need, or a serious illness, of course it will have to be shared. But there is no need to compare that child to the others because the goal is to understand that child's situation. In such discussions, the other children may, on their own, compare themselves to the "special" child. When this happens, parents may do best simply to listen. The goal would be to help the children understand what the comparisons *they* make mean to them.

For example, an older brother may compare himself to a younger sister who is gifted in math: "I'll never be as good at it as she is, and she's younger!" Parents might be tempted to minimize his concern, or to offer pat reassurances. Instead, find out why that bothers him, what it means to him. Eventually, he may come around to recognizing that he, too, has unique strengths, and that his sister has other shortcomings. The goal, of course, is for the siblings to accept themselves, and one another, as they are.

Competition in School

In school, one sibling's labels may be handed down to the next child. Though teachers usually won't say this, it can be hard for them not to think, for example, "He's the brother of that noisy kid. I guess he'll be noisy, too." A teacher might say to a gifted child's younger sibling, "He was one of the smartest kids I ever taught. I hope you're just like him."

Labels

It is, of course, natural, for teachers to connect each child with their impressions of the child's family. Teachers may feel that they can use labels to mark the family's individuality, or to start a relationship with an otherwise unknown child. They may rely on labels at first as they try to learn about each child. Labels, though, can become self-fulfilling prophecies. Expecting one sibling to follow in an older one's footsteps may sometimes open doors, but it can also be destructive. Each child in a family will want to feel that she has opened her own doors and left her own mark at her school. Can we limit labeling in schools and help siblings deal with labeling when it can't be prevented?

My 5-year-old granddaughter was placed in a class that her older brother had been in two years earlier. On the first day, the teacher said, "I hope you're as nice as Willie was. He was always on time and so helpful." My granddaughter replied simply, "I'm Addie." Addie would not be held to her brother's classroom behavior—good or bad.

Parents can be aware of the likelihood of labeling in school, and be ready to talk to the child about it after school: "She's great to remember Willie, and she wants to know you. Until she does, she may think you'll be like him. She won't have to do that when she's gotten to know you. Then she'll like you for yourself. You and he are so different, and she'll find out."

Schoolmates may label siblings, too. Younger siblings may have heard from older ones about the big brother or sister of the child in their class. Older children, too, may have heard about a classmate's younger sibling. Parents can expect this when one of their children stands out, whether with a special talent or a special need. Other children may ask, cruelly, whether a child is going to be "a retard, like your big brother," or expect a younger child to be a football star, too, or even embarrass a child whose younger sibling has succeeded where he hasn't.

Parents can prepare a child for this, and listen carefully for the child's feelings. It will be important for the child to know that even if the kids at school make comparisons, parents don't: "Kids at school may think they know you just because they know your big brother. But all you have to be is yourself."

Competition Between Siblings

This is inevitable: "She was in the school play and I wasn't." Or, "I'm in the advanced reading class, and you weren't." A younger sibling may ask an older sibling, "How did you do in math when you were in third grade?"

At my children's school, no one was ever given a grade. This was the school's attempt to reduce competition for grades and to value each child's individuality. (Later, the children would find that this sheltering had left them unprepared for their sudden introduction to competition upon entering high school.) Even without the grades, though, the children were already categorizing each other. One child bragged: "Everyone knows who's the best in math. Only a couple were better than me." Her sibling replied, "I did better than that when I was in your class. Only Alex was better than me."

This kind of competition is inevitable. Is it hurtful? Probably not, as long as it comes from the children, and as long as the balance isn't always tipped against the same child. If competition is intensified by adults' comparisons, fixed expectations for a child can lead to self-fulfilling prophecies and to destructive behavioral patterns among the children. Adults—parents and teachers—all need to look closely for subtle ways that they may be encouraging more successful children to lord it over the others, and for opportunities to support and encourage the less successful ones.

A Chance to Succeed

So often, opportunities for recognition in school are limited to a few narrow traditions—academic prizes, team sports, school plays, and the like. Schools sometimes introduce a wider range of activities (art, music, community service, mentoring children in younger classes, noncompetitive physical activities) so that every child can have the experience of excelling in something. If schools do not offer this, parents can encourage each sibling to try out all kinds of skills without feeling they must live up to an older sibling's successes in the same area.

Most stars of school plays and sports teams do not go on to professional careers in these areas. Both parents and schools would do well also to recognize children for other skills that they should be encouraged to take with them into their futures. These include academic ones, but also, for example, the ability to work as team, and to show altruism and compassion.

What Parents Can Do

If one child is struggling in a class that was easy for an older sibling, parents will need to pay attention. If there is an important reason for this new problem, such as a learning disability, the younger child's challenge can be made even harder by the older sibling's successes. It will be important to face the problem straight on, rather than to minimize it.

Parents and teachers can strive to avoid comparing the child to the older sibling. But when the child brings it up, listen, and take these feelings seriously. "Of course it doesn't seem fair for you to have to work so hard. Once you find your own special way of learning, you can do your best. And we will help you."

Parents can play down the natural competition in schools. They can focus on a child's areas of strength, and on such non-competitive qualities as being a good friend. (Kindness has become an underrated virtue in our world.) They can watch for labels, for self-fulfilling prophecies and the behavior it can set up in their children. "You seem worried about how they are treating you in school. Are they comparing you to your sister? Tell me about it."

If the child can let you know his feelings about following in his sister's footsteps, it could be an opportunity to back him up for his own individuality. If it becomes an issue over time, it might warrant a discussion with the teacher. Parents can describe their individual child. Each one deserves to have her identity recognized. A sensitive teacher will try to know and care about each child without making comparisons with another sibling.

Criticism and Praise

All children are hungry for their parents' approval. As a result, parents know they can use criticism to curb unwanted behaviors, and praise to encourage others. Sometimes, though, parents may not always realize just how seriously a child takes each criticism, each encouraging word. When other siblings become an audience, parents' words take on even more power. Praising one child can feel like a criticism of another; similarly, criticizing one can certainly seem like praise to another.

When there is an imbalance over time—more criticism for one child, more praise for the other—the criticized child is likely to give up and behave as "bad" as everyone seems to think she is. The child who must bear the brunt of parents' continual criticism also becomes the brunt of a sibling's: "You're a loser." A sibling will rub it in, glad not to be the brunt himself.

Praise, too, can be uncomfortable for the sibling who receives it, especially if the others are around. The praised sibling's successes then seem to come at the expense of the others. If a child such as this feels guilty, or is the target of jealousy and resentment, she might even stop trying so hard, preferring to be less special and more like the others.

Praise from a parent can easily be overdone. The child knows when it's phony. Too much praise from a parent can interfere with a child's learning to take satisfaction in his successes on his own. Yet praise can be a boost, particularly if it is fair and comes out of the blue. From a parent it is valued, but even more from a sibling. When an older sibling can praise a younger one and say, for example, "You did such a good job. You worked and worked at it"—think how proud both will feel. A younger sibling is likely to praise his older sister with his eyes, and with imitation. Is it wise to comment on their praise and take it away from them?

If you must criticize, avoid words such as "always" and "never." Rather than negative generalizations such as "You're never ready on time," focus on what's happening now: "You're late. We need to get going."

Teaching Self-Criticism, Self-Praise

Be careful about using praise or criticism as a way of controlling behavior. Either one can quickly feel like a weapon to a child. Your long-term goal is not this kind of power. Instead, it is to help your child learn to face his own strengths and weaknesses, to praise and criticize himself as he learns to monitor his own behavior.

Instead of saying, "Great job!" there may be a chance to ask: "How do you feel about how you did?" Your smile and warm voice tell her how proud you are, but you leave your child room to find her own pride. The added benefit of this approach is that siblings are less likely to feel that your approval of this child takes away from your approval of them.

The same goes for criticism. Of course there are times when a child needs to be told very clearly that she's made a mistake. But look for opportunities to ask her what she thinks she's done wrong, what she thinks she could have done better. A conversation like this is best carried out when the other children aren't around to add to her embarrassment.

Privacy Vs. Public Humiliation

Whenever possible, reserve criticism and sanctions for private times with a child. If the others ask, "How come you didn't punish her?" a parent can answer, "That's up to me, and it's between your sister and me." When the other children are present, stick to clear expectations and instructions that apply to all.

When siblings, or siblings and friends get out of control, there's no need to single one out. Tell the whole group, "You need to settle down." The others may protest: "But Susie started it!" Simply answer, "I'm not interested in who did it. I'm asking you all to help out." They'll get the message. Singling out a child for public humiliation, on the other hand, strikes terror in the hearts of children. But it won't win you their respect. To protect themselves from it, they're likely to turn against you.

Often, you may not know what really happened, or who started it. But when only some are guilty, all can still be helped to face their responsibility. This approach sustains a parent's authority while encouraging the children to recognize their interdependence. They may all turn against one sibling, but over time they'll learn to stick up for each other—an important goal for the whole family.

Disciplining Siblings

Can discipline be the same for different children? Not always. Is it fair to treat them differently? They won't think so, and they'll be playing close attention. But of course it may be, because they are different. Differences in discipline depend on age differences, differences in ability, sensitivity, and temperament. Siblings will reproach parents: "You're always so much easier on her than you are on me." I would advise parents to lay out their reasons openly so that differences in discipline won't be seen as playing favorites: "Do you really think it would be fair to treat you alike? You're three years older."

Parents may also find that they discipline their boys and girls differently, or they may do so without realizing it. Many will naturally soften to speak to a girl, and are more likely to be tougher with a boy. Will boys see this as unfair? Probably. Parents will need to stop and consider whether their different responses to a boy and a girl really fit the child or, instead, are based on a stereotype.

Fair discipline does not necessarily mean the same discipline for all. If different children really need different kinds of discipline to be contained and to learn from it, all the children can be helped to understand and accept this.

What happens when two or more siblings are involved? When they gang up to make a ruckus that you must stop? An older child may set up a younger one to do his dirty work because he's more likely to "get off easy." Sometimes, parents may know that the mischief goes beyond the younger child's abilities. Sometimes they won't.

What should you do?

- First of all, parents will need to get themselves under control.

- Then, address both children together. This is their chance to learn that they're all in it together as a family.
- Afterwards, separate each child for individual discipline—in private.
- Finally, bring the children back together again. Remind them that they are all responsible for each other, even when only one is guilty. Then, plan for a family time—a meal, reading together, a walk, or anything else that is warm and allows everyone to feel close again.

Separation from each other has the powerful effect of getting each child to listen to the teaching that goes with discipline, and defuses the excitement of ganging up on a parent. It also makes them realize how much they want to be together, no matter how upset they've been with each other.

When children keep misbehaving, over and over, either they've not yet learned from your discipline or the motive to misbehave is stronger. It is essential to help children discover their own motivation to get along with each other and to comply with the family's rules and expectations. Then they can begin to assume some responsibility for self-discipline. If this doesn't happen, siblings are likely to find it far more rewarding to gang up against parents and to goad each other to test parents' patience and resolve. When you can, turn it back to them and make the misbehavior their problem, not yours.

Another possibility is that your response has not been consistent. If you respond on some occasions, and not on others,

Fair and Appropriate Discipline

1. First of all, the punishment should fit the crime.
2. When you find yourself spending a lot of time disciplining your children for fights and rivalry, stop and consider how much to leave to them. They'll be more likely to listen if they haven't heard you nagging for a while.
3. Balance positives with the negatives. When your children are quietly getting along or working on their own projects, surprise them with a word of praise.
4. When problem behavior happens too often, ask the children what would help them behave. Let them plan solutions together.
5. Don't compare one child to another.
6. Don't talk about one child to the others.
7. Don't humiliate one child in front of the others.
8. Discipline is best absorbed by a child when it can be done in private. But it often happens that two or more children need it at the same time. You can remind them as a group of expectations and consequences that apply to all of them, without singling anyone out.
9. It takes a juggler to match the discipline to the child. A parent who knows each child's temperament, stage of development, learning style, and thresholds has a better chance. Watch her face and body movements for evidence that you are reaching her.
10. Be sure you find a positive word or activity afterward to balance out necessary discipline.

children are bound to keep on testing. They need to find out whether or not you'll respond next time. If you mean business, show them by responding the same way, every time. But don't get worked up about it. That may make the misbehavior even more exciting, and hard to resist.

Favorites

"She reminds me of my mother." "He's just like I was at that age." There are all kinds of reasons why a parent may favor one child over the others. Birth order, gender, a child's appearance, the way she moves, her spirit or temperament. Often, one child brings out unconscious reactions in parents over which they have little control.

Parents generally intend to treat children fairly, but it doesn't always happen. And the other siblings know it. "Why does Mommy's voice always get soft when she talks about Maddie?" When both parents dote on the same child, it can set up a dilemma for the other children. Or when a couple's arguments are always over the same child, it becomes all too apparent to the other children.

Favoritism, even unspoken and unrecognized by the parent, can undermine the other siblings' self-esteem. They feel like failures in relation to the favored child. If they feel that no matter what they do, they can't live up to the "special" one, they may give up trying and proceed to behave badly in a desperate bid for any kind of attention. Or they may look for adults who value them more.

I knew that my mother had a special bond with my younger brother. She'd spend hours trying to feed him, hovering over him. I was lucky in the end. I turned to my grandmother, who adored me. I was her first grandchild. She said delicious things to me: "Berry, you're so good with babies. You love people, don't you?" I still can hear her voice. All children need a backup person who admires them.

When a child is a favorite at home, she learns certain patterns of behavior. She may learn how to "work a room," to woo

---

What Parents Can Do to Avoid Playing Favorites

- Face your reactions.
- Attempt to equalize these reactions by getting to know the other children better. Spend extra time alone with each one.
- Value their differences.
- Emphasize their areas of competence—to them and to yourself.
- Talk in private with the other parent about each child. When parents fight over a child, even one they both favor, the child will be drawn in, and may get hurt.
- If your relationship with one child is difficult, try to provide another adult or young person who can become that child's mentor and cheerleader.

each adult individually. She becomes accustomed to the favored role. When she uses her charm on her peers, though, it is often less successful. She will have to learn to listen to them and take the focus off herself.

Fights

Fights may seem to be a constant in most families. Siblings know they can call a parent into their battle if they scream loud enough for help. But, as you know by now, whenever you enter their battle, you are upping the odds that they'll keep on fighting, and actually hurt each other. When you intervene, you are joining their battle, becoming a part of it, adding more intensity to the rivalry between the children.

Here are a few guidelines that can help:

A baby younger than 18 months and not yet physically able to protect himself or effectively reach out for help needs your protection. Each time the older sibling endangers him, sit down with the older one and say, "I just can't let you hurt him. You can resent him. You can tease him. You can get away from him. But you can't hurt him. You and I would feel too awful if you did. I'll stop you each time until you can stop yourself." When you give the older child permission to have such feelings, and show that you accept them, she will be less angry with everyone—you, her sibling, herself—and she will be less likely to hurt the younger sibling.

When all the children are old enough to protect themselves from being physically harmed by the others, it is wise to make it clear: "It's your battle, not mine. You need to learn to settle your own battles without me." When you show them that you respect them by saying, "You can work this out yourselves," they'll be motivated to rise to the occasion.

If you do have to intervene because one child is out of control, be sure to comfort each of them—one for the frightening feeling of losing control, the other for needing more help in learning how to stand up for himself.

Fighting with anything sharp or heavy can be dangerous. Usually, if both children are old enough to protect themselves, one sibling is unlikely to hurt another seriously unless a parent or a responsible adult is nearby. When there is no adult present to ensure that siblings will be "safe" if they lose control, the chances of their getting out of hand and hurting each other are diminished. They sense that their safety must be their responsibility.

Once children are old enough not to need constant watching, staying out of sight can be a good idea, though an adult still needs to stay near enough to hear real trouble. When no adult is in sight, most children realize they'll have to control themselves. No child wants to get hurt. And, with the exception of very disturbed children, no child really means to hurt others seriously—even if he or she "feels like killing him." Without an adult hovering, each sibling is more likely to feel a responsibility for the other child. Fights go on, but limits are set on how far they can go.

When an adult steps in, there is an implicit message: "I can't rely on you to stop yourself." One child slugs another. The victim screams but doesn't defend himself. The parent steps in, but in doing so may well be reinforcing a victim's role for the second child. Parents will want to consider these risks as they assess whether it is necessary to step in. Sometimes it is, for example, when a much stronger or much older sibling (four or more years older) repeatedly fights physically with a younger child, or, for example, when one child repeatedly exposes the other sibling's vulnerabilities in an intentional effort to humiliate that child. In their struggles, siblings usually exhibit a back and forth, a give and take. They take turns at "winning" or at "being on top." But when there is a clear imbalance of power, a parent will need to step in.

When it is necessary for a parent to intervene, it will be important to keep from giving the older or stronger child more to be angry about, more fuel for her fights. Talk with that child about herself, not the other child: "When you get out of control like this, I'll have to help you." And to the victim: "You are going to need to learn to protect yourself. You may have to learn how to get away from her for now. But you're going to get bigger and strong enough to protect yourself, too."

Both children need comforting. But the goal is to let one know that she can control herself and the other learn ways of protecting himself when others are out of control. In our dangerous world, every child needs to feel that she can defend herself. It may be worth considering lessons in self-defense. A child becomes more self-assured when she knows she can protect herself. A child who feels secure in this way is less likely to get into physical fights with siblings. (See *Mastering Anger and Aggression: The Brazelton Way* in the *Bibliography*.)

When to Worry

Throughout this book, we've made the case that sibling rivalry is natural and unavoidable, though parents can either make it worse or help keep it from escalating. Most often, staying out of it is the best bet. But there will be times when parents may need to take action.

Here are a few of the warning signs and situations that will require a parental response, and in some cases, professional mental health assistance as well:

When a Child Is in Danger of Physical, Sexual, or Emotional Abuse.   Abuse is different from expectable sibling squabbles. Siblings who abuse another will seem not to care about the child they hurt. They will be unable to put themselves in that child's position, nor will they be able to imagine what it feels like to be abused. They are often driven by anger. They are likely to rationalize what they are doing as somehow justifiable, or as serving a purpose. Playfulness, nurturing, and remorse will be painfully absent.

The abused child is likely to be too frightened and compliant to ask for help from parents. She may have been threatened with worse treatment for speaking up. Sadly, this kind of sibling relationship often occurs when parents are caught up in their own overwhelming struggles. It can seem as if the children have been infected by their anger, and as if the parents are too weighed down by their own emotions to see what is happening to the children.

Dangerous Physical or Emotional Violence.   Sometimes the danger is in the degree or severity of the assault. For example, although siblings will inevitably hit, kick, bite, and scratch, normally they'll stop before they cause serious harm, and they won't use potentially dangerous objects or weapons to hurt each other. Throwing heavy objects at each other, threatening with scissors are already over the line.

Repeat Attacks.   Sometimes the danger is less obvious. The attacks do not seem as serious, but the damage comes from the constant repetition. When one sibling bullies over and over, the sibling who is the victim will take on the identity of a victim, potentially damaging the development of his personality. Usual sibling tussles involve more balance, more back and forth, with children taking turns in different roles. The stronger, older child who attacks on one occasion ought to be nurturing and kind on another. The younger, more vulnerable child might be paralyzed with helplessness on one occasion, but ought to fight back or assert himself to get help the next time.

When Everyone Is Angry.   When children take out their anger on kids outside the family, the behavior may be a sign that they are also bullying younger siblings at home, or that an older sibling is tormenting them. Both can happen when children feel discouraged and inadequate, or have not learned how to handle their anger. It can also occur when parents are unable to handle theirs. This is particularly likely when there are too many pressures on the family, or when parents' own problems interfere with their availability and overwhelm their self control.

What to Do?

First, look at your own responses to your children's fights. Might you be reinforcing their anger with each other without knowing it, perhaps by comparing or criticizing? Second, consider each child's current situation. Are there any reasons why a child might be filled with anger that overflows onto a brother or sister? Perhaps the child has no friends at school, or is the victim of bullying there; maybe he is failing at school and feeling insecure, or he worries about parents' fighting, and so forth. These are the kinds of things that you may be able to address with each child. But in your attempt to adjust and balance, you may find yourself caught in a trap—as you try to support or protect one sibling, the others just grow angrier and intensify their attacks. Because siblings' struggles so often arise from feelings about their parents, help from a mental health professional who is a family outsider can make all the difference.

Gender Differences

Parents' feelings about gender so often underlie their reactions to a child. Most often, parents have positive associations with the gender of a favored child, whether it is their own gender or not. Sometimes, a child of the same sex as a parent reminds that parent of distressing past experiences, creating negative, gender-based feelings about that child. Parents need to be aware of such feelings so that they won't be at the mercy of them. Siblings will recognize a parent's differing reactions to gender, in themselves or in their playmates, and may model on them.

When there are many children, but all but one are girls, or all but one boys, the lone child's gender is bound to be an issue. If everyone makes a fuss, this lone child's gender identification will be heightened—a "girlie girl" or a "little tough guy" may be the result. If not, the child is likely to try to fit in with the others, and will absorb as much as possible from them. A boy in a family of girls may be more aware of his "feminine side." If he imitates his sisters, his father may react with disgust. This will only push the boy closer to them. A girl in a family of boys may be more likely to be a tomboy.

"I had three brothers and didn't know anything about girls," one woman explains. "All the neighbors' kids were boys. No wonder I turned out this way." Because she had been a tomboy as a child, she says, she became an EMT, fixes everything herself, and moves the filing cabinets in her office before the movers come. She was the second of four children, but I doubt that mattered as much as her being the only girl.

On the other hand, her two younger brothers were born five years after her, and she was like their "little mother." Now she has six children of her own and has raised scores of foster children. It does seem likely that her younger two brothers taught her to nurture, and to value nurturing. When there are two brothers or two sisters, the feelings of competition can be intense. Closeness may more often be experienced in conflict, and positive feelings are more likely to be hidden.

Relationships between siblings of opposite genders may be more comfortable. It can be easier for a child to relate to a sibling of the other gender. They are not in competition for the same role, so may present less of a threat. Two such siblings often will identify more intensely with their own genders as a way of distinguishing themselves from each other, the "slotting" effect we discussed in Chapter Two. Parents will want to take care not to push siblings of different genders further into stereotypical roles, while valuing, of course, their genuine differences.

Gifted Child

How does it feel to be a sibling in a family when there is an "exceptional" child—an artist, a musician, an athlete, a straight "A" student? The "exceptional" child stands out. Everyone else admires her. Parents bask in her glories. "We never thought *we* could have such a bright child. Where does her talent come from? Certainly not from me!"

Everyone treats the child as a miracle. No one treats her like the other children. If they did, she might lose that miraculous shine. Adults pay attention to every word, and repeat them with reverence. Nothing she does is handled in the same way as for the other children. The child herself may have a feeling of unreality. "Am I normal? What do they really feel about me?"

Such a child is likely to feel she has to strive to live up to these fantasies of specialness. She may not feel she can turn to her parents for guidance or to share a moment of weakness. When she does, they behave as if she knew better than they. When she makes a mistake or misbehaves, everyone is so surprised and disappointed, and she feels so ashamed. It's not easy to be a "special kid." The limelight doesn't allow for play, mistakes, and mediocre performance.

Under pressure to be "special," the child may become a perfectionist, putting herself under even more pressure. Peers are likely to be jealous or awed, or both. They may shun her, or treat her so specially that normal friendships are almost impossible. The give and take of friendships can be rare experiences for exceptional children. The pedestal quickly becomes a lonely place.

When a gifted child compares the way she is treated to the way her siblings are treated, she may feel uncomfortable: "It makes me feel funny." On the other hand, it's also exciting to be special. It takes a lot of self-control not to lord it over siblings when they are easily surpassed. But siblings offer the gifted child the longed for chance to "just be normal."

Siblings of such a child are bound to be aware of the difference in the treatment she receives from everyone. They see the gifted child's accomplishments as something they should try to attain, but there is a kind of hopelessness attached to these wishes. Their self-esteem may be in danger.

A parent of a gifted child may be so caught up in that child's accomplishments that the other siblings feel rejected. Parents in this situation need to understand the predictable striving and self-devaluing of the other children, and to make extra efforts to value the strengths in each of them. Parents need to look for and treasure the differences of the other siblings. Let the other siblings talk about how they feel about the gifted child: "I get sick of hearing about how great she is. It makes me feel like a worm."

At that point, parents can draw them out to say more about these negative feelings instead of sweeping them under the rug by prematurely reassuring them. Then, parents can encourage them to talk about qualities in themselves that they can be proud of, for example, being a good friend, persistence, endurance, as well as their own academic, athletic, or artistic abilities. Helping the siblings to recognize their own gifts, without condescension, is one of the most important things a parent can do. Another is to provide the other siblings with the support and resources they need to develop their own talents.

Discipline is bound to be different for the gifted child and her siblings. For some gifted children, discipline may be almost nonexistent. Some may be expected to recognize and set their own limits. What does this special treatment cost a child? It's almost as if she weren't a child. No one expects her to play normally, or to need the help that most children need. If no one offers the reassurance of discipline, the child who isn't disciplined doesn't feel loved.

The need for discipline for every sibling can't be ignored. The sibling of a gifted child may say, "But, Mom, you let Miss Special do it. It's not fair." You can reassure him that there are rules for the gifted child as well, and that both he and "Miss Special" have to learn to discipline themselves.

Family times are important for a gifted child. Eating meals together and playing together become even more important. The gifted child needs a family around her. She needs those times to be "just like the others"—as much as she can. Siblings need to experience the equal treatment that these family times demand.

Gifts

"Shouldn't I get something for my oldest since everyone's bringing gifts for our 1-year-old's birthday?" parents often wonder. Giving a gift to one child can almost seem like taking something away from the others. Should a parent give smaller, token gifts to the other siblings—on a birthday or other special occasion?

Parents may feel the need to calm siblings' jealousy when they see one child receiving so much. But for the child being honored, these efforts may seem to take away from the special status she expects from her celebration. Such feelings can be expected, and parents can plan their response in advance.

For a younger child (up to 3 or 4 years), a small gift can help keep him from interfering with a sibling's special celebration, such as a birthday. Maybe the birthday child could participate in picking out the gifts. "She knew it would be such a great day for her that she wanted to share it with you. She got you this gift."

When children are older, though, such occasions are important times for them to learn to step aside and hand over the spotlight to a sibling. It is also a chance for them to learn to handle their feelings of jealousy and frustration as they watch a sibling open all the presents and they are left empty handed.

One 4-year-old whose mother was about to give birth to a new baby brother watched the preparations for his arrival intently. When friends sent a big package for the baby containing a white teddy bear bigger than the baby would be, the 4-year-old immediately grabbed it and announced that it was hers. She named it "White Cloud." Her parents, already feeling guilty about "abandoning" her for the new baby, couldn't bear to set her straight. She'd never wanted a teddy bear before, but she took this one to bed and held it tight every night, for years—until she left home for college! Fortunately, her brother gave her many other chances to learn to share and to sacrifice over the years. Her parents always wondered whether they should have helped her learn that she couldn't always have everything she wanted the day White Cloud arrived. I would have advised them that this was not a time to face that challenge. The birth of a baby is one special occasion when an older sibling needs support rather than pushing when she falls back on younger ways.

At holidays such as Christmas and Hanukah, all the children receive gifts, compare their "loot," and either gloat or feel slighted. These feelings can't be avoided entirely, nor need they be, as children will need to learn to handle them. But they can interfere with the importance of these holidays as times for the family to enjoy being together.

Despite parents' efforts, rivalry and jealousy will peak at these times. Help children prepare for such overwhelming feelings and discuss them in advance. "Everyone looks forward to Christmas for so long that they can feel disappointed when it finally comes. Sometimes you get exactly what you want, and sometimes you don't. Worst of all, sometimes it seems that everyone else gets all the good stuff, and you don't get what you wanted. It feels so yucky it could wreck the whole holiday. But that wouldn't be worth it, would it?" Watching siblings receive gifts that are "theirs," and accepting that these are "not mine," is a necessary part of learning how to share and value others. The goal, after all, is for the child to discover the satisfaction of giving.

Large Families

Not surprisingly, experiences of siblings in a larger family are often very different from those in a small one. The first and the last children clearly have special roles in a large family. But if you look closely, so do all the children in the middle. Gender and age differences, along with temperament, often make for unique roles for each child, and distinct relationships between one sibling and another. Often, they all will have to learn self-reliance. But they'll also learn to rely on each other, to carry on many unique relationships at the same time. They'll learn about themselves from the others.

They know they are a group and they are proud of it. When rivalry surfaces, it is either handled within the group or shoved underground. At times, though, their pride in the pack may be balanced by other feelings: "I get so sick of my brothers and sisters. They're always around. I wish I could be on my own." Some may actually relish the chance to be alone. Others will quickly find that they long to be together with their siblings again. To some extent, this will depend on how parents handle their interactions and their individuality.

One woman we know, now in her fifties, was the fifth of eight children, and the only girl. "Daddy made sure we all were at dinner together every night. We went around the table and he asked each of us about our day. Each of us had this time to be special to him. When one of us got in trouble we all paid the price. If it was one kid's fault, sure we'd be mad. But only for a little while, because we all knew that it could have been any of us. So we'd always end up sticking up for each other. That was what Daddy wanted." To this day, she and her brothers all live within a few miles of each other. At Christmas, more than a hundred children, grandchildren, and cousins turn out at her father's house.

Sometimes, one child in a big family calls up a parent's own memories and past experiences. This may become the child's way of attracting special attention—good or bad. For example, my wife had been a third daughter. She identified closely with our own third daughter. She thought she knew what our daughter was experiencing and thinking. The other children knew it and cried out from time to time: "You treat her so special!" It didn't seem to me that she was treated differently. But there was a particular bond between the two, left over from my wife's own past.

Special Relationships

Often each sibling has a special favorite sibling in the family and shows it. Sometimes it's based on gender, sometimes it's based on temperament, sometimes it's based on birth order. But often it seems to be none of those. Siblings who choose each other in this way seem to depend on each other—turning to each other first when they're in trouble, and for daily confidences.

When one sibling is emotionally unstable or seems difficult for peers to accept, siblings in a large, nurturing family may step in and try to fill the gap. Siblings often have a special bond with such a child, and an uncanny understanding of her needs, and how to reach her. I remember the parent of a 3-year-old with autism who always brought one of the older siblings with him to my office. "He'll do all kinds of things for his brother that he won't do for me or you." There are, though, times when this may not happen. Then, the troubled child may feel alone at home as well as with peers. When a child seems always to be on the sidelines, or routinely scapegoated, parents should seek professional help for that child.

Rivalry in Large Families

Sibling rivalry may seem to be submerged under the daily hub-bub. But it isn't. The rivalry in large families may be just as intense as it is in small families. It may even be magnified at times if the other siblings take sides. The meltdowns are just as disruptive, but when only two of the siblings are involved, no one else may pay much attention. Still, two siblings may tease and torture each

---

Calming Rivalry in Large Families

1. Remember the closeness and mutual dependence that lies beneath sibling struggles.
2. Watch for the nurturing the older ones have learned from you. Praise them.
3. Try to make a special time for each child once a week, a "date" with one parent or the other when nothing can interfere with it. It need not be very long, but it must be a kept promise.
4. Regular family meals bring a family together. Keep television out of these precious times for closeness.
5. Plan family meetings to share ideas, gripes, rewards. Lay out the family chores and let each child choose one. When siblings argue about chores, let them plan fair solutions. "Do you think leaving all the clean up to just one of you seems fair?" or "Do *you* like it when all the toys are a mess?"

other to raise so much commotion in a large family that the parents have no choice but to step in. When they finally break up the headlocks of two enraged siblings, the exhaustion and the overload of the parents is likely to surface. If the other children have not taken sides, the parents can more easily separate these two and set them to tending chores with a different brother or sister.

Miscarriages

Parents often want to believe that their children didn't really know about a miscarriage. They want to spare them the sadness and confusion. But children of all ages are likely to have been aware of a pregnancy. Even if they are not told, very young children can tell that something important and different is happening. Children recognize the differences in the behavior of a pregnant mother from the beginning. They feel the mood of celebration in the father.

Often parents have already shared their excitement about a pregnancy: "You're going to have a brother" or, slyly, "You are going to have a new playmate soon." The family will build up to the coming event. When the pregnancy comes to a sudden disappointing stop, the parents are bound to mourn.

A sibling will feel both sadness and curiosity. "What happened to Mommy? Why won't we get a new baby?" And lurking behind their identification with their parents' grief is their own question: "Did I cause it? Did something I did get rid of that baby? Did my wishing—not to have one—come true?"

A child may be on "best behavior" if she feels responsible. As long as parents grieve, she may be "too good," as if waiting for parents to recover before letting herself fall apart. Or she may behave badly to see whether her grieving parents can tolerate her in spite of the loss, as if to persuade them to snap back into shape and be emotionally available to her again.

The depth and duration of the child's reaction is bound to be tied to the length of the pregnancy, the amount of talking about the baby that has occurred, and whether siblings can comfort each other while their parents grieve. A miscarriage is especially hard to grieve, for parents and for siblings, because the seriousness of the loss is often unrecognized. Outside the family, the miscarriage will not be treated as if it were a major event, though family members may very well grieve as they would for a death.

It is especially important for parents to offer simple, clear information about what happened, and to be available for the children's questions. A parent might say, "I have something very sad to tell you. The little egg that was growing inside me died. It stopped growing, so my body couldn't keep it inside me anymore."

The children are bound to ask, "Why?" Tell them what you know in a way that they can understand, or let them know that you don't have all the answers you want, either. "No one knows what happened for sure. Sometimes there is a problem with the baby's body before it is born so that it won't be able to live. It is sad that this baby could not live, but maybe it is better that it died before it had to suffer."

Let them know they can ask questions, whether you know the answers or not. They may feel they must keep questions to themselves for fear of making you break down. Let them know it's okay if you do, that you'll all feel sad, but that you can also pull yourselves together.

Only Child

Many parents today realize that having more than one child would stretch their resources beyond their capacity. Others, who have a first child late, may not be able to have a second pregnancy. When both parents must work, or a parent is raising children alone, the cost of childcare often limits the number of children a family can have. And today, many parents feel that one child is the right choice in an overpopulated world.

At the same time, parents may have concerns for that child. They know they are putting all their eggs in one basket. Although their devotion to that one child may be a boon for the child, it can be hard not to become overprotective, to spoil her, or to push her to grow up too soon. An only child may respond to her parents' heightened expectations by excelling beyond her peers. But without siblings to dilute the pressure, a child could become overwhelmed, or rebel.

Parents of only children can make a conscious effort to avoid over-praising and over-protecting. They can seek opportunities to help their child learn self-reliance. Discipline is essential, and it's reassuring to an only child. An only child may ask for a sibling to play with. She may dream of a sister to "baby." Instead, parents will have to find ways to show her how to share her toys and her parents with others, and to learn how to be part of an extended family.

Play dates, visits with cousins, and preschool will all help an only child learn to share toys and to make friends. Loneliness may be a powerful force driving her to learn new social skills. Parents can model generosity for a child who hasn't had to adjust daily to siblings' needs and offer her opportunities to discover the rewards of giving.

Caring for the Only Child

1. Look for and value the child's unique temperament and individuality.
2. Don't try to change her or push her to be perfect.
3. Avoid over praising. Let her learn how to value herself.
4. Be careful not to over-protect your only child.
5. Gradually allow her to try out new people, and new activities with new demands and risks that correspond to her growing abilities.
6. Get together with other parents for advice and to gain perspective on your expectations.
7. Foster your child's friendships. Make regular play dates. Start these with future classmates before they enter a new school together. Help them find activities that they both can become involved in. Close friends are especially important for an only child.
8. Whenever possible, let your child get to know her cousins, or the children of your closest friends, so as to give her the feeling of belonging to a family or community.

Parents of an only child need to take socialization seriously. Find a peer who is like your child in temperament. Then, woo her. Take them together to museums and playgrounds, for example, for regular play dates. In advance of a friend's visit, help your child by setting out toys that you both agree can be shared. Talk about the rules of sharing ahead of time so that she can get along with her new playmate. It is critical for an only child to have a friend. Having one helps an only child make the transition to a group setting, such as school, and to be accepted by other children of her age.

Parents who were themselves only children may say: "I was an only child and I never learned how to be like other children." Or they may feel that once they entered school they were just like everyone else. Only children need the help of friends who can accept them. Parents who from experience understand the unique challenges of the only child can help their child learn how to live with others, just as they themselves have learned.

Scapegoats

Scapegoats are blamed for things that aren't their fault. Whenever people are unable to accept their own responsibility for a problem, or don't want to pay the price of admitting it, they look for a scapegoat. One U.S. president, trying to handle his defeat for a second term with dignity, said, "Thank God my mother taught me not to blame anybody else for my own shortcomings!"

A ready-made scapegoat has flaws that everyone already knows about. This knowledge can come in handy for siblings. Just exaggerate a sibling's shortcomings and, soon enough, everything will be her fault. Blame her for everything, over and over, and her shortcomings protect the others from responsibility. She's a perfect scapegoat.

No one will listen if the scapegoat tries to defend herself—she is needed too much in this role. The more she's blamed, the less the others would ever want to be in her position. They'll work even harder to keep her on the hot seat, and to protect themselves from humiliation. Worse, the scapegoat may come to believe that all the nasty gossip about her is true.

Whenever a child is labeled—"always late," "messy," "trouble maker"—the siblings will begin to echo the labels. "She always makes a mess everywhere she goes." The child begins to see herself as messy: "I know everyone thinks I'm messy." So why bother to change? Unconsciously, she begins to act out this image of herself. It becomes a part of her character. She'll even set herself up to be blamed and criticized, and won't dare to stand up for herself. She has stepped into the victim role.

The scapegoat label carries with it a self-fulfilling prophecy. A famous experiment separated white rats, all the same, into two cages. One cage was labeled "Smart Rats." The other was labeled "Dumb Rats." Graduate students put them through a maze. More smart rats got through the maze than dumb ones. Meanwhile, the graduate students' treatment of the rats had been captured on film. They handled the rats entirely differently, as might be expected. A "smart" rat was coddled and placed gently into the maze. A "dumb" rat was picked up roughly by the tail, dropped into the maze, and couldn't get oriented. The kind of treatment the rats received determined whether they would succeed or fail. The same thing happens to scapegoats.

Parents need to watch for this kind of labeling and to balance criticism with encouragement and acceptance of the child. "You can be messy, but we can help out with it. Let's all pick up together." Parents need to remember that modeling is the most powerful way of teaching their children. If they can be aware of and stop their own scapegoating of one child, they are more likely to break the cycle for that child.

Parents can look for opportunities to help the child change her behavior. "I see your face change when you mess up. I know you don't want to. When you say how sorry you are, I know how much you mean it. Maybe I can help you next time, even before it happens. Maybe you can tell me what would help you. When we all jump on you, it just makes it worse for you."

Siblings who succeed in shoving one child into being the family scapegoat will also suffer. They'll know when they're exaggerating, and they'll see the child's pain. To avoid guilty feelings, which can be lasting, they'll work hard to convince themselves that the scapegoat's plight is deserved. Parents can help all the children by helping them face their responsibilities. "I know you all get annoyed with your sister. But you can also tell how badly she feels when we all gang up on her, and I know it bothers you to see her feel that way." The other children may be slow to admit that they do care, but they'll come around if parents don't push them too hard into facing their feelings.

Still, parents will need to let the children know what scapegoating is, and that it won't be tolerated. If they find that the same child always seems to be in trouble, parents will need to find ways to balance their criticism of this child. Parents can show all the children that they mean business by spreading out responsibility, rather than always singling out one child to be blamed. Parents' responses to bad behavior must demonstrate to all the children that if they find fault in others, they must also face their own role. Even if one child did nothing to cause a problem, she must ask herself whether she did anything to try to prevent it. Scapegoating can be stopped when children understand that although only some may be guilty, all are responsible. It may take time.

Sexual Exploration

Sexual exploration and play are common among young siblings. As they are bathed together in infancy and toddlerhood, siblings are bound to look at and touch each others' genitals. Before the age of 3 or 4 years, their interest will soon shift back to splashing and sailing their plastic boats. Three-year-olds love to ask, "Why?"—perhaps even more than they like hearing the answer. "Why does she have *that,* and I don't?" You might try Mr. Rogers's answer: "Boys are fancy on the outside. Girls are fancy on the inside." "Why does his wee-wee stick up like that?" You might answer, "It's very sensitive. Sometimes it sticks up when it feels something different, or when it feels nice." Watch the children's faces to see whether you've gone over their heads with your answers. Their eyes will glaze over and they will turn back to their toys when they've had enough.

As they grow older, such exploration may capture their attention for longer and grow more intense. At the ages of 4 and 5, children become aware of differences and want to understand them. Children of this age are bound to experiment with each others' bodies, touching each others' private parts as they make up stories about "playing doctor." The more openly their questions to you are handled, and the more comfortable you are in answering them, the less likely they are to become preoccupied with such experimentation. So be prepared (see Robie Harris's books for explaining sexuality to children, listed in the *Bibliography*).

By now, they may be ready for separate bath times, and for the concept of privacy. "Your body is special, and so is his. Yours is just for you to touch, and his is just for him to touch." When siblings of this age start showing a preference for "doctor play," it is also time for you to introduce a variety of other play activities for them, including ones in more public places—outdoors, or in the living room or kitchen. By the age of 6 or 7, most children lose interest in sex play with siblings, and often find the whole idea "disgusting."

When to Worry

Normally, sexual exploration or play between young siblings involves equally willing participants. When it occurs between siblings 4 or more years apart, such mutual agreement is not possible. Their needs and ways of understanding are too different. The younger child is easily coerced, or ready to agree to anything to admire an idolized much older sibling. Even with a smaller age gap, evidence of coercion means the sex play must be stopped.

Sexual exploration is a child's way of finding out about her own body and other children's bodies. But there are so many other things a child must explore and learn about through her play. When sex play becomes a regular activity, and a major focus for siblings' play, then it is time to intervene. Redirecting them to other activities, and being more available as a parent when they are together will help. If they have been secretive about sex play, they probably already feel guilty. They won't need to be made to feel more so. You will also want to consider why the children have become so preoccupied with sex play. It may be that they are bored, need other kinds of stimulation, and more supervision.

Sexual exploration and play in young siblings should be childlike. They may look and touch, but if they use their mouths and genitals in such interaction as adults do, then it is likely that their own sexuality has been interfered with by that of an adult. When children's sex play resembles adult sexual behavior, the children may have been exposed to pornographic material, witnessed adults engaged in sexual acts, or even been sexually abused by an adult or older child. Other signs include changes in a child's behavior that are typical of sexual abuse, for example, distress when using the bathroom, taking a bath, changing clothes, and at bedtime, or frequent sexual self-stimulation and sexual preoccupations. If you have concerns about your child's sexual behavior, talk with your pediatrician. He or she can help you determine whether specialized evaluation and treatment is necessary, and will refer you to a mental health professional for this if needed.

Sharing Rooms and Space

Whether children share rooms is determined by necessity. In many cultures, children share rooms and sometimes beds with each other. It pushes their closeness, and even their rivalry, to be faced more openly, and their relationships may be more intense. We are fortunate if we can provide a room for each child, but it isn't always possible. As puberty approaches, though, children of different genders are bound to insist on more separation.

If possible, be sure that each child has an area and a time for privacy. Privacy is not only critical for creating respect for each other's bodies but also for letting off steam and enabling each child to recover from the pressures of living so closely with other siblings. Private space can help a child maintain a balance of control over his strong feelings and his impulses. Even when sharing a bedroom, each child can have a space of her own, her shelves or a bureau, for toys and valuables. A sheet or curtain can be hung from the ceiling to provide some privacy. When children are old enough to be trusted to be safe in bunk beds, these can be a great way to keep them close, but separate, and to open up more space for their private corners in a shared room.

When a second child is born, you may want to keep the baby in your room until he has learned to sleep through the night. Later, if one child routinely wakes up during the night to awaken the other, you might consider taking the child who has already learned how to sleep through the night independently into your room. That way, the other child can awaken and learn to put himself back to sleep without having a roommate to wake up. Be sure, though, that neither one sees the separation as a punishment.

Many adults have fond memories of sharing rooms and even beds together. Nighttime is such a precious time for sharing confidences. Two brothers, now grown men with families of their own, told me of sharing a bed until they were adolescents and the eldest was sent off to boarding school. They both missed the closeness, and keeping each other warm. In addition to lacking separate bedrooms for all the children, their house had been without central heating! Now their families are close and share vacations together. We sometimes hear from adults who grew up in very large houses that they felt isolated and alone, even lost. They, too, look for closeness in their families as adults, but often seem to have trouble knowing how to find it, or how to enjoy it when they do. When children must share living space, they have an opportunity to learn to share, to respect, and to be close.

Sibling with Special Needs

A child with special needs presses the whole family into service. Not only are the parents' lives at the mercy of caring for the special child, but the siblings must adjust to this major demand on the family system. If the child is receiving early intervention (the earlier the better) or other treatments, parents can ask for advice and support to help the siblings adapt. Some treatment centers offer groups for siblings of children with special needs. In these groups they can discover that they are not the only ones who feel the way they do, from sad and scared to bitter and jealous. There, these feelings can be spoken aloud, and accepted. Each family must face these challenges in their own way—but they need not be alone. Find someone who can help the whole family.

The specific nature of the child's impairment is critical to understanding the stresses on the siblings. A child who has an autistic spectrum disorder, for example, has difficulty relating to others. As a result, she may be very difficult for siblings to understand. Frustration is to be expected. "Why won't she play with me, or look at me, or talk to me? I don't like her. Can we get rid of her and get another baby instead?"

Siblings often express what no adult dares even to think. A child with special needs can be embarrassing to her siblings. They may not dare bring friends home. They may think, "If it can happen to her, will it happen to me? We're the same family. My friends will think I'm weird, too." As horrifying as their comments may sound, a parent's ready ear is far better than leaving siblings to handle such negative feelings on their own. The siblings need to ventilate their disappointment and anger with an understanding and accepting parent.

A child of normal intelligence and social abilities who is paralyzed, unable to walk, or has severe coordination impairment (as with cerebral palsy) knows that she's not developing like her siblings. This can be very hard for her and she may explode with frustration and anguish. The siblings may begin to hold back or to hide their accomplishments. On the other hand, they may be motivated to special achievements to try to please their stressed parents and somehow "balance out" the sibling's disabilities. If this happens, it is important for siblings to understand the nature of the disability and to realize that the child has many skills and talents that are not affected.

Parents need to help siblings understand the reasons for the special child's delay, her limitations, and her strengths. They'll also need to remember that the healthy child may be blaming herself. Communication and listening for the siblings' questions and misunderstandings is critical.

Often, all the family's energy must go into the special child's treatment. Everyone concentrates on each step in the special child's development. "When will she begin to walk? I help her a lot." Or, "She won't talk. I yell at her when Mom's not around, but she just won't talk." Beneath this focus is the undying question: "Will she ever be normal?" It is so hard to accept that all the wishing and all the work in the world can't cure certain disabilities.

If a mother and father are in mourning, or busy providing constant care to a child with a disability, they may be difficult to reach. A sibling may have to misbehave to provoke attention. The siblings naturally have stored up their anger at how much this one child demands. When something bad happens, there'd better be someone to blame: "Everyone in my family works so hard to help her. But she just won't help herself. I wish we didn't have her and could just be a normal family."

Children may also blame the parents for bringing this burden into their lives. A small child needs to blame someone. At times it will be her parents, at others, herself. Children of 4 and 5 years will take everything personally. "I didn't want her to come to our house. It's my fault she's so messed up."

Many siblings of children with special needs learn to turn their guilt into altruism. They may go into helping professions—medicine, occupational or physical therapy, psychology. Their experience has led them to learn how to help others. They may also become athletes or scholars, driven by a need to prove themselves. The challenge faced by the whole family can lead the child with special needs, as well as her siblings, to discover deep reservoirs of strength.

Spacing

Ideally, couples can decide in advance about the spacing of children. Today, parents will also want to decide how our planet's population problem will influence the size of the family they plan. Unfortunately, such decisions may not always work out as hoped. Some types of contraception are not foolproof, and as couples grow older, their reproductive systems may not always be cooperative.

Breastfeeding mothers who rely on the hormonal changes of nursing as a contraceptive may be surprised by a second baby, born just a year or so after the first. They are both still babies, but of different ages and with different demands. This is exhausting, particularly when it is unexpected. Parents of twins or two babies close in age spend the first years in constant motion. No one sleeps. No one sits down to eat. No recovery time.

Even if they are very different from each other—in temperament, intensity, or gender, these siblings are likely to grow up almost as close as twins. They'll look out for each other. They'll take everything that happens to the other personally. If you reprimand one, the other may burst out crying. By the third year, their closeness will become a major asset. They will have learned to take care of each other. The other side of the same sibling coin—competition—is always there, too.

Their rivalry can be intense. Their fights never end. But if you, as a parent, can leave their rivalry to them, they are likely to be fairly matched in each battle, and they learn so much about survival!

When a child reaches the age of 2, it becomes easier to introduce a sibling. The older one will be able to protest and even push away his baby "adversary." At 2, he has all these ways of expressing himself—and his feelings about the baby—openly. But he won't yet have much ability to suppress these feelings. It all sounds daunting, but in the long run, the siblings are likely to be friends and close enough in age to be treated as a "team." As parents, you can look forward to a time free of diapers, and, not too far off, to when both children are in school. Later, it will be easier, with this closer spacing, to find family activities for weekends and vacations that both children will want to participate in. Mothers or fathers who take time off work to be with small children may choose to have children close together.

Some experts have concluded that 4 to 5 years apart may be the "ideal" spacing. The older child will have experienced her babyhood to its fullest. She will be ready for some independence and is likely to model on the mothering she sees lavished on her new baby. She'll be more interested in her peers than in the new baby. A 5-year-old can be nurturing and a big help with the baby from time to time. Of course, she, too, will be angry—with you, and the baby—for making her share you. But a 5-year-old has more control over her angry impulses, and more effective ways to cope with the sadness she'll feel at being "deserted" by you. Best of all, you'll never have to worry about more than one college tuition bill at a time!

A baby born to older parents, or a "surprise baby" at the end of the line, may be especially prized. However, after a few nights of lost sleep, you may start wishing you were younger. If there are older children, this last one can be a real gift. But don't expect them to thank you, no matter how much older they are. Still, they can help. They can watch him learn new tasks. He can be the lucky recipient of the older siblings' attention. They can make him the center of all the laughs in the family. However, if they are in their early teens, they may be embarrassed by the sexuality that a pregnant mother represents. As teenagers, they may grouse more about responsibilities for nurturing a baby sibling, even if privately they enjoy it. Parents are often surprised by how jealous much older siblings can be, and by how much attention from them their teenagers still need.

Stepsiblings and Half-Siblings

As children adjust to "siblings" from another family that is being "blended" with their own, they must face new and unexpected obstacles.

A Child's "New Mother"

If it's the father who has remarried, the new mother may exclude the father's children at times when nurturing occasions arise. At mealtime, the father's children may watch who sits next to her to see who gets the first serving from her. They may try to woo the mother instead of waiting for her to reach out. They may make a lot out of each little sign. They're bound to feel unequal to the stepmother's children, or, later, to children born of this second marriage. As a result, they may try to please their stepmother *or* they may turn against their half-siblings, criticize them, and isolate themselves.

A Child's "New Father"

When it's a new father who comes into the family with his children, the mother's children may behave quite differently. They may resent their stepfather or they may try to woo him. But they'll also realize that he has his "own children" to please. They are likely to tease or fight or try to put stepsiblings down. The other children are bound to fight back or to tattle, putting mother and stepfather in an awkward position. How will they handle a fight between stepsiblings?

Visitation

The timing, frequency, and length of visits with the "blended family" will have powerful effects. The longer a child spends with her stepsiblings, the more likely she and they will learn to become friends. This will also be more likely if parents can help all the children feel that they can share their "own" parent without giving up on their own special relationship to that parent.

If the siblings can't get along, the parents who have brought them together will discover that they can't impose their own wishes on the children's stressed relationships: It won't work to say, "You have to like her. She's your sister now." A child is bound to reply, "Oh, no, she's not. She'll never be. I hate her."

Some children may not feel that they can express themselves so candidly for fear of losing a parent. "If one parent will leave me, will the other?" As if to prevent this, she must suppress her negative feelings about the new siblings as well as she can. It may work, but it may not. She may feel even more anger about losing her own family and then having to fit in to this one. "I never asked for a stepbrother. It's not fair. I don't like him. I hate my parents for making me do this." She'll wonder how to retaliate against stepsiblings, stepparent, or parent without anyone's knowing. She may learn underhanded maneuvers to work out some of her negative feelings.

When parent and stepparent have a biological child together, everything is likely to change. The new baby becomes a symbol of the parents' commitment to their new marriage. Meanwhile, the other children may feel as if they were reminders of mistakes and marriages left behind. The children of divorce recognize that they are in a more vulnerable position. They may compete with the new child, or they may not dare to. Resentment is bound to underlie their acceptance of the new baby. I would advise parents to expect such feelings, and to give the children permission to voice them. They'll also want to listen for the children's hidden concerns. "Have I lost my parent again? Must I be perfect to be loved as much as the baby?"

From Comparisons to Accepting Differences

Stepsiblings naturally compare their families with each other. "My mother gives me so much freedom. You should see. She never makes me go to bed at night. Not like you have to here. I wish I didn't have to come here to be with all you guys." Or, "My stepfather is always there when I go to be with my mother. He has pesky little kids and I have to babysit. I really hate that." Comparisons in each child's mind are bound to color the sibling relationships. They are likely to throw these comparisons in each other's faces.

What can a parent do? You can't change your children's feelings. When they express them, they are working on adapting to this new reality. You can help them by letting them know you are ready to listen, and that you care about how hard it is for them. This can be difficult for parents who've just come through a painful divorce and wish they could just leave it all behind. But you can't, nor can your children. They are bound to be making comparisons between their own families and their stepfamilies. It's a way of learning about and accepting their changed lives.

Competition and Closeness

Competitive feelings are bound to arise—more so in blended families—when there are events that focus all the attention on one child, such as birthdays or special performances. Visitations to a nonresident parent, crises, stress on the family or on a particular child are also bound to heighten angry competitive feelings among stepsiblings.

When something goes wrong, it may seem like a punishment. A child who already feels responsible for her parents' divorce now has stepsiblings and a stepparent she can conveniently blame to protect herself from her guilty feelings.

Living in a stepfamily is not easy. Everyone is vulnerable. The more honest parents can be between themselves about how they feel about their own children and each other's, the more effectively they can respond to all the children. Parents are bound to think that they should feel the same way about their own children and their stepchildren. But they don't. By sharing their different feelings with each other, parents in a blended family can support each other and work toward being fair and understanding with the children.

Stepparents are not and never will be the same as parents. They needn't try so hard to behave as if they were. This only reinforces their differences in attachment. "I love you and care deeply for you. But I am your stepfather, not your father. You have a father of your own, just as my children have me. All of you children can work out your own struggles with each other. You don't have to love each other, but you do have to live with each other."

If the parents join solidly together in expecting the children to learn to live together, it helps. If parents take sides—to protect their own—they will be more likely to fuel the children's

Fostering Strong Stepsibling Relationships

- Show that you expect them to learn to live together. They don't have to love each other.
- Assure stepchildren that you aren't going to try to be their parent, but that you can care about them.
- Give them permission to feel differently about their stepsiblings.
- If a parent buys gifts only for his biological children, it will cause jealous feelings. Anticipate this. But don't overdo trying to make up for it.
- Parents—resident and nonresident—need to agree as much as possible with each other on discipline, expectations, on predictable challenges such as bedtime, and on issues that are bound to stir up jealousy, such as giving presents. This is difficult in the face of old, unresolved hostility, but it will surely help the sibling relationships and the feeling of family. It smoothes out the transitions as a child goes from one household to the other.
- Separate rooms for separate sexes as much as is possible. Often the children of each parent may want to live together in separate rooms. Try it, when possible, until they learn more about each other and learn to care. Then, they may be ready to share a room. But don't rush to break up the special closeness of each sibling group.

competition and bullying. Stepparents will usually need to leave limits, discipline, and important decisions up to the living-in biological parent.

A child learning to adjust to a new stepfamily is bound to play one parent against the other, and may even take advantage of a parent's feelings about the other children to do this. If you can see through this instead of reacting, you'll be able to help the child face his angry feelings and begin to build relationships with the new stepfamily.

Twins and Multiples

Different and the Same

The intensely passionate ties that exist between twins and multiples often come as a surprise to parents. They may expect them to be more competitive. But they are always amazed by the different "slots," or roles, each one takes. One is likely to be active and out there. The other is a watcher, quiet and sensitive.

Even identical twins seem to set up these contrasting personalities. They're never identical in behavior. It's almost as if they were fitting their roles to each other like a jigsaw puzzle. When one performs, the other is either watching carefully or matching her twin's rhythms.

Learning from Each Other

Twins seem to take turns at playing dominant roles. When one is more adept in physical activity, that one will be dominant in the first year as they both develop motor skills. The less dominant one watches, watches, watches the other's movements, and then imitates them. She seems to have learned visually from the more physically active one, who has had to put the activity together in steps.

As they grow from one stage to the next, twins may take turns in taking the lead for learning. The active twin practices a new motor skill, such as learning to stand and walk. Up and down, up and down, learning to balance with one hand on the chair holding on. After a month or more of practice, she finally dares to let go. She staggers across the room and plops down on her bottom, her face glowing with her success at taking a few, free steps.

Meanwhile, the observer twin has been watching her struggle. Babbling to encourage her, she brightens with her sister's new achievement as if it were her own. For the next few days, she watches hungrily as her sister adds more and more mastery to this new skill. As if she'd learned from watching, the observer twin puts it all together, pulls up on a chair, lets go, and staggers across the room—all at once, without ever having practiced! Her active teacher twin looks up at her and gurgles in approval. They walk toward each other to fall in a heap—just as they'd always slept at night, an arm across each other, touching each other's stomach or buttocks.

When they enter the second year and language is becoming more important, the quieter one may take over. Her language skills become highly prized and she leads her twin into sentences—in the same way that she was led by her sister's physical activity. The less dominant one—in this area—learns in hunks rather than one word at a time, imitating the strings of words her sister has figured out how to put together. The more verbal one puts words together: "Mama, home!" The more active one stops, listens, and tries to imitate. This switching of dominance seems to be a safe way to equalize their dependence and to enhance their deep relationship.

I learned a great deal about language development from a pair of 2-year-old Japanese twins. They were quiet, gentle little girls, and I was very surprised when their mother complained to me that she couldn't ever persuade a babysitter to come back a second time. I urged her to stay around the corner before she went out to see why they were so "difficult." She called me the next day. "They have a special language with each other when I go. Every word is half Japanese and half English. No one can understand it. Who wouldn't feel left out?" These quiet little girls had developed their own barrier to intrusions into their intense relationship.

A Special Closeness

The intense attachment of twins and multiples is so remarkable that it causes jealous responses in those around them. A sibling will try to pull them apart, physically or emotionally. Unable to, she may resort to complaining: "The twins! They *have* to do everything together. If I play with one, I get both." A parent watches this love affair with unspoken, even unconscious feelings of being excluded. "Should I separate them at night? Maybe they're too close, too dependent on each other."

The emotional tie that twins and multiples develop seems to go deeper than anything any of the rest of us has ever experienced. It's no wonder that so many authorities (teachers and others) are always pushing to separate them. But why shouldn't twins and multiples stick together?

Time to Separate?

When the twins enter a school setting, parents may feel that they should be in separate classes, should have separate friends. Is this a reflection of the parents' concern for the intensity of their relationship, or is it their own unrecognized competition with each child for closeness with the other? My answer would be a question: "Are the children ready to separate?" Until then, why separate them? They depend on each other. They learn so much from each other. It's such an admirable, secure relationship. Why indeed would one want to shake it?

Eventually, they'll want to separate, but not until at least 4 or 5 years. At these ages, they are likely to begin to want their own friends, their own clothes. Then will be the time to support their own wishes to emphasize their differences. It isn't an easy transition. They are likely to try to have separate friendships, but when stressed, they'll return to each other. I have seen a 5-year-old twin moan over not having his twin to play with. When one twin is hurt, the other reflects the pain. They are still joined at the hip.

One 6-year-old worried all day when his twin sister had to stay home from school with what seemed—to everyone else—to be a minor cold. He begged his teacher to call his mother. "I'm worried about Annie." That afternoon, his mother took his twin to see the doctor, who diagnosed pneumonia. Twins will always know each other better than anyone else.

Competition and Separation

Sooner or later, competition between the twins arises. Everyone expects it. Maybe the rest of the family even reinforces it. When a twin lunges for a toy, someone might say, "Don't let him have it!" When one twin bites the other playfully, his siblings say, "Davey, don't let him do it. Fight back." Watch the soulful, sad eyes of the biter as he registers that he's hurt his beloved twin.

Though parents expect the competition, they are surprised by the angry feelings, and the intensity of the passion twins may show as they struggle with each other. Their deep bond is, of course, on the other side of the coin. But the switching back and forth of the dominant role in the first few years has started the process of their becoming individuals. As they develop the awareness of themselves as actors in the world, competitive and angry feelings are bound to surface. The intensity of these feelings reflects how difficult it is for them to separate from each other. After a scrap, parents need to comfort them both. Parents can reassure themselves that maintaining the twins' relationship, not separating them, is the more important goal.

Bibliography

Books for Parents

Brazelton, T. B., and J. D. Sparrow. *Touchpoints Three to Six: Your Child's Emotional and Behavioral Development.* Cambridge, Mass.: Perseus, 2001.

_____. *Discipline: The Brazelton Way.* Cambridge, Mass.: Perseus, 2003.

_____. *Sleep: The Brazelton Way.* Cambridge, Mass.: Perseus, 2003.

_____. *Toilet Training: The Brazelton Way.* Cambridge, Mass.: Da Capo, 2004.

_____. *Mastering Anger and Aggression: The Brazelton Way.* Cambridge, Mass.: Da Capo, 2005.

Conley, Dalton. *The Pecking Order: Which Siblings Succeed and Why.* New York: Pantheon, 2004.

Hannibal, Mary. *Good Parenting Through Your Divorce.* New York: Marlowe & Co., 2002.

Hetherrington, Mavis, and John Kelly. *For Better or For Worse, Divorce Reconsidered.* New York: W. W. Norton & Co., 2002.

Rufo, Marcel. *Frères et Soeurs: Une Maladie d'Amour.* Paris: Fayard, 2002.

Sulloway, Frank. *Born to Rebel.* New York: Vintage, 1997.

Trozzi, Maria. *Talking with Children About Loss.* New York: Penguin Putnam, Inc., 1999.

Wallace, Meri. *Birth Order Blues.* New York: Henry Holt and Co., 1999.

Wallerstein, Judith. *The Unexpected Legacy of Divorce: The Twenty-Five-Year Landmark Study.* Hyperion, 2001.

Books for Children

Harris, Robie. *It's So Amazing: A Book About Eggs, Sperm, Birth, Babies, and Families.* Cambridge, Mass.: Candlewick, 1999.

_____. *Hi New Baby!* Cambridge, Mass.: Candlewick, 2000.

_____. *Happy Birthday.* Cambridge, Mass.: Candlewick, 2002.

_____. *Hello Bennie: What It's Like to Be a Baby.* New York: Simon and Schuster, McElderry Books, 2002.

_____. *Sweet Jasmine, Nice Jackson! What It's Like to Be Two and to Be Twins.* New York: Simon and Schuster, McElderry Books, 2003.

Kellogg, Steven. *Much Bigger than Martin.* New York: Puffin, 1992.

McCloskey, Robert. *Blueberries for Sal.* New York: Puffin, 1976.

_____. *One Morning in Maine.* New York: Puffin, 1976.

Videotapes

Touchpoints: Your Child's Emotional and Behavioral Development. A three-part series by T. B. Brazelton. Available from the Brazelton Touchpoints Project, www.touchpoints.org.

Index

About the Authors

T. Berry Brazelton, M.D., founder of the Child Development Unit at Children's Hospital Boston, is Clinical Professor of Pediatrics Emeritus at Harvard Medical School. His many important and popular books include the internationally best-selling *Touchpoints* and *Infants and Mothers.* A practicing pediatrician and leading advocate for children for more than forty-five years, Dr. Brazelton has also created the Brazelton Touchpoints Project (www.touchpoints.org) to support child development training for healthcare and educational professionals around the world.

Joshua D. Sparrow, M.D., is Assistant Professor of Psychiatry at Harvard Medical School and Special Initiatives Director at the Brazelton Touchpoints Center. He is the co-author, with Dr. Brazelton, of *Touchpoints Three to Six;* and the *Brazelton Way* series on *Calming Your Fussy Baby; Sleep; Discipline; Toilet Training; Feeding Your Child;* and *Mastering Anger and Aggression.*